Chairman Mao's
Business School

Chairman Mao's Business School

Lars Kleivan

To order additional copies of this book, contact:
Xlibris Corporation
1-888-795-4274
www.Xlibris.com
Orders@Xlibris.com
32676

Dedication

To my late brother-in-law—Odd Stener Kristiansen and my wife Kari-Brit.

Mao Zedong—A Short Biography

Mao Zedong (1893-1976), Chinese statesman, founder and chairman (1949-76) of The People's Republic of China. Mao became a member of the Chinese Communist Party in 1921. After the nationalist Kuomintang, led by Chiang Kai-shek, dissolved the alliance with the communists in 1927, Mao helped establish rural soviets. In 1931 he was elected chairman of the Soviet Republics of China, based in Jiangsu. The advance of nationalist forces forced Mao to lead the Red Army on the Long March (1934-35) NW to Shanxi. In 1937 the Civil War was suspended as communists and nationalists combined to fight the second Sino-Japanese War. The communists' brand of guerilla warfare gained hold of much of rural China. Civil War was restarted in 1945, and by 1949 the nationalists had been driven out of mainland China. Mao became chairman of The People's Republic of China and was re-elected in 1954. Zhou Enlai acted as prime minister. In 1958 Mao attempted to distinguish Chinese communism from its Soviet counterpart by launching The Great Leap Forward. The program ended in mass starvation and the withdrawal of Soviet aid. Mao's leadership was challenged. The Cultural Revolution was an attempt by Mao and his wife—Jiang Qing, to reassert Maoist ideology. The cult of the personality was encouraged, political rivals were dismissed and Mao became supreme commander of the nation and the army (1970). Mao and Zhou Enlai's death created a power vacuum. A struggle developed between the Gang of Four, Hua Guoffeng, and Deng Xiaoping. Quotations from Chairman Mao Zedong (popularly known as "The Little Red Book", 1976), is a worldwide bestseller.

Philips World Encyclopedia

CONTENTS

I

Introduction

What did Mao Say?

Things develop ceaselessly. It is only forty-five years since the revolution of 1911, but the face of China has completely changed. In another forty-five years, in the year 2001, or the beginning of the 21st century, China will have undergone an even greater change. She will have become a powerful socialist industrial country. And that is as it should be. China is a land with an area of 9.600.000 square kilometers and a population of 600 million people, and she ought to have made a greater contribution to humanity. Her contribution over a long period has been far too small. For this we are regretful. But we must be modest—not only now, but forty-five years hence as well. We should always be modest. In our international relations, we Chinese people should get rid of great-power chauvinism, resolutely, thoroughly, wholly and completely.

"In commemoration of Dr. Sun Yat-sen"
(November 1956). LRB 179.

Chairman Mao Zedong wrote a number of books, made thousands of speeches and wrote numerous articles. Unlike what you hear from or read by most politicians these days, the content of these books, speeches and articles were full of pragmatic and moral guidance as to the way his empire should be run and controlled. With close to 700 million inhabitants during his period of reign, 6 provinces, 26 regions and a large number of prefects, counties, municipalities etc., this indeed was not an easy task. However, his books, speeches and articles were full of wisdom—and I stress wisdom—as to how the Chinese nation should be run efficiently. This wisdom was gathered in his

Little Red Book that was published for the first time in 1957 and altogether has been printed in billions of copies—second only to the Bible. The book contains 427 quotations in 33 thematic chapters.

These statements and quotations were intended to be practical guidelines for generals, soldiers, political leaders, civic leaders, teachers, business leaders (to the extent that they had any) and the common man in the type of system that existed at that time. This was during the Cultural Revolution—which lasted from 1966 to 1976. At that time China was a communist state with entirely different goals than what the country has today. But in order to attain their goals there was a need for organization and principles of leadership as we have in the political and business world. I believe that most of us would reckon that the principles of management that Mao urged his fellow Chinese to apply are entirely different from the principles of management that we practice in the western world. However, to my amazement they are rather similar. If you read Mao's Little Red Book with quotations and replace words like soldiers with workers, generals with CEOs, party cells with departments, cadres with middle management, armies with companies, masses with customers or employees etc., you will see that Mao had a brilliant insight into the areas of organisational and management science. He devised methods that apply just as well to the management of a company or an organization in the western world as to the management of his vast empire, which was a formidable managerial task.

Chairman Mao was a revolutionary with grand political goals and visions. Business managers who are successful are often small or large revolutionaries themselves. They have bigtime ideas, visions and goals. They realize them with vigor, endurance, perseverance, assertiveness, charisma and often relentlessness. Most of all they believe strongly in what they are aiming at. Very often their personal lives are full of sacrifices, often at the expense of their closest family. While they often drive their staff hard, they have the ability to enthuse and empower their men and women so that they became their loyal followers—like great generals in wars. These are some of the reasons that I strongly believe that it will be useful for the coming generations of managers in all types of countries to study what Chairman Mao said in different contexts and relate them to the daily life of small and large corporations.

This book is not a discussion nor an endorsement of the politics that Chairman Mao carried out during his years in power.

The Little Red Book has a format of 3,5" x 5,1" (9 cm x13 cm). Its cover is made of red plastic and the little book fitted well into the pockets of the millions of red guardians that were instrumental in carrying through the Cultural Revolution in this vast country. They brought it with them on their journeys around in the country; the idea was to spread the credo of the Cultural Revolution to the entire Chinese population.

The following excerpts from the foreword of the Little Red Book describe how Lin Piao recommended that the book should be used:

> " . . . . In studying the works of Chairman Mao, one should have specific problems in mind. Study and apply his works in a creative way, combine study with application, first study what must urgently be applied so as to get quick results, and strive hard to apply what one is studying. In order really to master Mao Zedongs's thought, it is essential to study many of Chairman Mao's basic concepts over and over again, and it is best to memorize important statements and study and apply them repeatedly. The newspapers should regularly carry quotations from Chairman Mao relevant to current issues for readers to study and apply. The experience of the broad masses in their creative study and application of Chairman Mao's works in the last few years has proved that to study selected quotations from Chairman Mao with specific problems in mind is a good way to learn Mao Zedong thoughts, a method conducive to quick results.
>
> We have compiled Quotations from Chairman Mao Zedong in order to help the broad masses learn Mao Zedong's thoughts more effectively. In organizing their study, units should select passages that are relevant to the situation, their tasks, the current thinking of their personnel, and the state of their work."

This is the way that I have written this book. I have tried to find quotations that fit situations in business and management and translated what Mao said to provide practical help for a modern manager. Many of the quotations apply to different areas and therefore you will find that some of the quotations are repeated. In some cases a part of a certain quotation fits one situation while another part of the same quotation suits another.

Below you will find a picture of the cover of the Little Red Book and an appeal to read it as well as the Table of Contents.

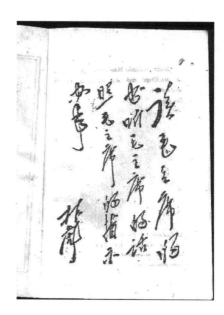

Study Chairman Mao's writings,
follow his teachings and act
according to his instructions.

The Table of Contents is as follows:

Most of the quotations relevant for business are found in the chapters that are written in bold.

Let me thus explain—to you who are in the process of building market economies in China or in any other country—how you can get spiritual and practical guidance from Chairman Mao's quotations. Combined with my own experience and the experience of other businessmen and -women I also hope that it will give ideas and inspiration to build corporations that will succeed in the competitive world—whether you are fighting for market-shares nationally or internationally. I want to show you how parts of his work are also a guide to the daily life of how to run a western-type company—particularly in the Scandinavian way. In Scandinavia we have a management style that is more democratic and involves and empowers employees to a larger extent in the decision-making process than in other cultures. To my great amazement and satisfaction I also note that this is an important part of Chairman Mao's philosophy as well.

This is not a science book. My intention is to give you an overview of the most important aspects of running a company. My experience—to my surprise and regret—is that the corporate world, with its small as well as large outfits, is neglecting a number of the basics that I am addressing as we proceed with this book. I am certain that focus on the points that I am addressing and implementation of the methods and ways of thinking will help significantly in building your company, making sure that you are not missing opportunities, and assuring that "black clouds" are being detected as early as possible so that you can be proactive and not only reactive. What I am describing is certainly not "rocket science". However, my experience is that simple approaches often do the trick and are certainly better than nothing. In the literature list, however, you will find a lot of sources for more detailed studies on the various subjects.

I am trying to make it a "cookbook" that in a simplified way gives you an overview of some basics that are extremely important when you manage a company or any organization. What I want is to help you develop your company along the paths that are described on the next pages. I want to give you advice as you go from today's situation to a prosperous future where you become an attractive proposition for your customers, your employees, your partners and your owners.

How to read this book?

When you read the quotations you will find a lot of words that are not particular business language. These words are those that you find to the left in the table below. To put them into your business context, exchange them with the words that you find to the right in the same table. In doing this I hope you find that you can adapt the quotations to meaningful business guidelines. I believe that many of them with these modifications more or less could be part of your company's ideological platform (See page 46)

o	Generals	President, General Managers, Managing Directors, CEOs
o	Officers	Management, top, middle
o	Committee	Functional management groups, committees
o	Cadres	First line managers—future middle and top managers
o	Fighters	Employees, salesmen
o	Troops	Employees, workers
o	Army	Business in general, the employees
o	Peasants	Employees, workers
o	Masses	Employees, workers, customers, markets
o	Party	The company, the business in general, the corporation
o	Squad	Department, division
o	Enemy	Competitors, those who possess what we want
o	War	A different war (one that is not fought with weapons and munitions)—competitive situation
o	Comrade	Fellow worker, colleague
o	Ideology	Mission, vision, values, policies
o	Nation	The company
o	Communists, socialists	

I have tried to write the book in a report style with short and efficient language, using graphs, pictures and tables to facilitate comprehension. Very often this is efficient from a learning point of view. I put important words in boldface type; I use indents and bullet points to give you easier access to my viewpoints. I have also tried to use analogies, metaphors and pictures to facilitate learning and to give you tools that will make it easier to communicate similar points to your followers. Quotations from Chairman Mao are written in italics and most of them are in a frame. Quotations from other sources are normally written in italics as well.

I recommend that you define a situation that you want to address. Find an appropriate quotation and adapt it to your situation. Let us assume that you want to create a personnel philosophy. Look up a quotation, f. ex. the following:

We must know how to take good care of the cadres. There are several ways of doing so.

First, *give them guidance. This means allowing them a free hand in their works so that they have the courage to assume responsibility and, at the same time giving them timely instructions so that, guided by the party's political line, they are able to make full use of their initiative.*

Second, *raise their level. This means educating them by giving them the opportunity to study so that they can enhance their theoretical understanding and their working ability.*

Third, *check up on their work, and help them sum up their experience, carry forward their achievements and correct their mistakes. To assign work without checking up and to take notice only when serious mistakes are made—that is not the way to take care of cadres.*

Fourth, *in general use the method of persuasion with cadres who have made mistakes, and help them to correct their mistakes. The method of struggle should be confined to those who make serious mistakes and nevertheless refuse to accept the guidance. Here patience is essential. It is wrong lightly to label people "opportunists" or lightly to begin "waging" struggle against them.*

Fifth, *help them with their difficulties. When cadres are in difficulty as a result of illness, straitened means, or domestic or other trouble, we must be sure to give them as much care as possible.*

This is to take good care of cadres.

Replace cadres with employees and see what you get. In my mind this is a good recipe for treating your employees and potential candidates for employment in your company. Anyone would yearn to work for a company with such a policy.

My humble vision or grand idea is to share some of my theoretical knowledge and practical experience with you so that **you** can be a better manager in the particular corporate context in which you are working. I also hope that it will give you an insight in some parts of China's history.

So—let's go or as Lin Piao said: *"Study Chairman Mao's writings. Follow his teachings and act according to his instructions"*.

II

How to be an Efficient Business Executive

What Did Mao Say?

Ask your subordinates about matters you don't understand or don't know, and do not lightly express your approval or disapproval . . . . We should never pretend to know what we don't know, we should "not feel ashamed to ask and learn from people below" and we should listen carefully to the views of the cadres at the lower levels. Be a pupil before you become a teacher; learn from the cadres at the lower levels before you issue orders. What the cadres at the lower levels say may or may not be correct; after hearing it we must analyse it. We must heed the correct views and act upon them . . . . Listen also to the mistaken views from below; it is wrong not to listen to them at all. Such views, however, are not to be acted upon but to be criticized.

"Methods of Work of Party Committees" (March 13, 1949),
Selected Works, Vol. IIIV, pp. 378-79. LRB 109.

Place the problems on the table. This should be done not only by the "squad leader", but by the committee members too. Do not talk behind people's backs. Whenever problems arise, place the problem on the table for discussion, take some decisions and the problems will be solved. If problems exist and are not put on the table, they will remain unsolved for a long time and even drag on for years. The "squad leader" and the committee members should show understanding in their relations with each other. Nothing is more important than mutual understanding, support and friendshipbetween the secretary and the committee members, between the Central Committee and its regional bureaus and the regional bureau and the area Party Committee.

"Methods of Work of Party Committees" (March 13, 1949), Selected Works,
Vol. IV, pp. 377-78. LRB 108.

We must learn to look at problems allsidedly, seeing the reverse as well as the obverse side of things. In given conditions, a bad thing can lead to good results and a good thing to bad results.

"On the Correct Handling of Contradictions Among the People"
(February 27, 1917) 1ˢᵗ pocket ed., pp 66-67. LRB 221.

A fact-finding meeting need not be large; from three to five or seven or eight people are enough. Ample time must be allowed and an outline for the investigation must be prepared; furthermore, one must personally ask questions, take notes and have discussion with those at the meeting. Therefore one certainly cannot make an investigation, or do it well, without zeal, a determination to direct one's eyes downward and a thirst for knowledge, and without shedding the ugly mantle of pretentiousness and becoming a willing pupil.

"Preface and Postscript to Rural Surveys" (March and April 1941).
Selected Works, Vol. III, p. 11. LRB 235.

In the sphere of organization, ensure democracy under centralized guidance. It should be done on the following lines:

1. *The leading body of the Party must give a correct line of guidance and find solutions when problems arise, in order to establish themselves as centres of leadership.*

2. *The higher bodies must be familiar with the situation in the lower bodies and with the life of the masses so as to have an objective basis for correct guidance.*

3. *No Party organization should make casual decisions in solving problems. Once a decision is reached it must be firmly carried out.*

4. *All decisions of any importance made by the Party's higher bodies must be promptly transmitted to the lower bodies and the party rank and file.*

5. *The lower bodies of the Party and the Party rank and file must discuss the higher bodies' directives in detail in order to understand their meaning thoroughly and decide on the methods of carrying them out.*

"On Correcting Mistaken Ideas in the Party" (December 1929).
Selected Works, Vol. I, p. 109. LRB 116.

Inner-Party criticism is a weapon for strengthening the Party organization and increasing its fighting capacity. In the Party organization of the Red Army, however, criticism is not always of this character and sometimes turns into personal attack. As a result, it damages the Party organization as well as individuals. This is a manifestation of petty-bourgeois individualism. The method of correction is to help Party members understand that the purpose of criticism is to increase the Party's fighting capacity in order to achieve victory in the class struggle and that it should not be used as a means of personal attack.

"On Correcting Mistaken Ideas in the Party" (December 1929).
Selected Works, Vol. I, p. 110. LRB 264.

Some Simple Rules to Improve Your Efficiency

As a business executive or one who aspires to be one, it is very important to have good work habits. In your job you will be exposed to a lot of pressure and if you have learned good work habits your ability to achieve more in less time will increase significantly. I am starting this book with this because my experience is that if you master this, your ability to survive and get ahead is significantly enhanced. There are two dimensions of this:

o   Start to use the types of technical tools that are available like PCs, PDAs, mobile and other telephones, conference call facilities, video-conferencing etc. Do not only learn their basic functions, but also the more advanced things that they can do for you and your organization. I am a strong contender of the fact that most users of modern technology are only to a small extent using the technical functions of their investments and very little of their software potential. The consequences of this are that the person or the organization that has invested in the equipment is getting a smaller return compared to the situation where the user is taking full advantage of the opportunities that the equipment offers. In other words, read the user manuals, call help desks, train yourself, attend courses and spend some time in understanding how to efficiently utilize what you have at your disposal.

o   The second dimension are things like discipline, orderliness, trustworthiness, time-management, meeting management, efficient planning of time, responsiveness etc.

Let's look at some of the aspects of this basic prerequisite for being an efficient executive or manager.

- **Be disciplined**

  Do all the things that are expected of you—make sure that you understand what these expectations are. Do not let things drag on. In other words avoid procrastination. If the decision is dragging out, you will waste time thinking about the matter, you will be handling it several times, in other words get it off your desk and/or mind before you are forced to make a quick decision because time has run out. Your reputation will also be damaged if you are considered a bottleneck in the system. Respect the requests that come from your colleagues, from the corporation, from other departments, from your customers etc. Try to meet deadlines. If you cannot, let those who are expecting your response know that you will be late. My experience is that those who are good at this advance more rapidly in the organization than those who aren't.

- **Delegate matters that somebody else in your organization can do for you**
  Avoid the factors that hinder delegation—remember that everybody—even you—has done a lot of things for the first time in their life. You should therefore have a tolerance for making mistakes and that things might take a little longer for the beginner. This is an important way of helping your subordinates to develop themselves. If they succeed you will also succeed. Therefore, learn the rules of delegation and use them actively to develop your staff.

- **Stay orderly**
  Keep your desk clean; learn how to organize the files on your computer; find a smart way to keep your paper files in a way that helps you to find documents quickly; keep your work files close to you; establish a reference file that contains the most important information that you need to access frequently. I also urge you to keep "To do" lists—first and foremost on your computer, but paper based "To do" lists are also ok. You can of course rely on your brain—but in the long run you won't forget as much with such lists as without.

- **Take Notes.**
  Buy yourself a little notebook or something similar in which you take down important things that come to mind—day or night. Do not only trust your memory. Use such a book to record the content of conversations, meetings etc. Take notes to demonstrate to those that you are listening to that you are attentive and interested. Be responsive and do something with

what you are hearing. This does not necessarily mean that you have to take positive action. If you don't, let those who are affected by your decision know that the matter will not be dealt with and explain why. Explain why you disagree. Also, use your notes to plan your time.

- **Plan your time**

  Use the "1/2 hour slots" as a Danish female minister with 11 children said when she was asked how she was able to manage to do all the things that were expected of her with such a large family. Do the most boring things first—when these are completed you will be filled with energy to do other more interesting and value-creating activities. Make sure that you do not fill up your calendar with meetings—allow for time at your desk, to relax, read and do paper work that is required of you.

- **Run meetings efficiently**

  Meetings take a lot of time—therefore there are some rules to be followed:

  - **Before the meeting**

    i.   Make sure that a meeting is really required
    ii. Call the meeting in writing
    iii. State the agenda
    iv. State clearly what the purpose of the meeting is—including what the expected outcome is so that the attendees have a chance to prepare themselves and determine whether their presence is required.
    v.   Ask people to confirm their attendance

  - **During the meeting**

    i.   Start the meeting on time—unless there are very good reasons for not doing so

ii. Appoint a person to chair the meeting

iii. Appoint a person to take notes and write the formal minutes

iv. Follow the agenda—bring the meeting back on track when it derails in relation to the point that you are dealing with

v. Make sure that one person speaks at a time

vi. Make sure that everybody is given a chance to voice their viewpoints

vii. When an agenda point is completed, make sure that there is a conclusion.

viii. Keep the time

ix. Use methods like brainstorming, mind-mapping and other creative techniques when it is appropriate. We will address these techniques on the following pages.

- **After the meeting**

  i. Write minutes after the meeting with the conclusion that states who is responsible and due dates if there are actions to be taken.

  ii. Distribute the minutes to the participants and other parties concerned.

- **Respect other people's time**

  - Ascertain that those you call to a meeting really need to be there.
  - Do not send letters to people to whom the content is irrelevant.
  - Do not copy people on letters unless it is absolutely necessary—do absolutely not do it to demonstrate to your boss that you have done what is expected of you, to cover your back etc.

Involve Your People to be Creative and Active in Problem Solving

What Did Mao Say?

The masses have boundless creative power. They can organize themselves and concentrate on places and branches of work where they can give full play to their energy; they can concentrate on production in breadth and depth and create more and more welfare undertakings themselves.

> Introductory note to "Surplus Labour Has Found a Way Out" (1955). The Sosialist upsurge in China's Countryside. Chinese ed., Vol II. LRB 119.

Take the ideas of the masses and concentrate them, then go to the masses, persevere in the ideas and carry them through, so as to form correct ideas of leadership, such is the basic method of leadership.

> "Some Questions Concerning Methods of Leadership" (June 1, 1943), Selected Works, Vol III, p. 120. LRB 128.

We should go to the masses and learn from them, synthesize their experiences into better, articulated principles and methods, then do propaganda among the masses and call upon them to put these principles and methods into practice so as to solve their problems and help them achieve liberation and happiness.

> "Get Organized!" (November 29, 1943), Selected Works, Vol. III, p. 158. LRB 129.

In all the practical work of our Party, all correct leadership is necessarily "from the masses, to the masses". This means take the ideas of the masses (scattered and unsystematic ideas) and concentrate them (through study turn them into concentrated and systematic ideas), then go to the masses and propagate and explain these ideas until the masses embrace them as their own, hold fast to them and translate them into action, and test the correctness of these ideas in such action. Then once again concentrate ideas from the masses and once again go to the masses so that the ideas are persevered in and carried through. And so on, over and over again in an endless spiral, with the ideas becoming more correct, more vital and richer each time. Such is the Marxist theory of knowledge.

> "Some Questions Concerning Methods of Leadership" (June 1, 1943), Selected Works, Vol. III, p. 119. LRB 128.

You can't solve a problem? Well, get down and investigate the present facts and its past history! When you have investigated the problem thoroughly, you will know how to solve it. Conclusions invariably come after investigation, and not before. Only a blockhead cudgels his brains on his own, or together with a group to "find a solution" or "evolve an idea" without making any investigation. It must be stressed that this cannot possibly lead to any effective solution or any good idea.

"Oppose Book Worship" (May 1930), 1st pocket ed. p. 2 LRB 233.

Investigations may be likened to the nine months of pregnancy, and solving a problem to the day of birth. To investigate a problem is indeed to solve it.

"Oppose Book Worship" (May 1930), 1st pocket ed. p. 3. LRB 233.

A fact-finding meeting need not be large; from three; to five or seven or eight people are enough. Ample time must be allowed and an outline for the investigation must be prepared; furthermore, one must personally ask questions, take notes and have discussion with those at the meeting. Therefore one certainly cannot make an investigation, or do it well, without zeal, a determination to direct one's eyes downward and a thirst for knowledge, and without shedding the ugly mantle of pretentiousness and becoming a willing pupil.

"Preface and Postscript to Rural Surveys" (March and April 1941). Selected Works, Vol. III, p. 12. LRB 235.

A commander's correct dispositions stem from his correct decisions, his correct decisions from his correct judgements, and his correct judgements stem from a thorough and necessary reconnaissance and from pondering on and piecing together the data of various kinds gathered through reconnaissance. He applies all possible and necessary methods of reconnaissance, and ponders on the information gathered about the enemy's situation, discarding the dross and selecting the essential, eliminating the false and retaining the true, proceeding from the one to the other and from the outside to the inside; then, he takes the conditions on his own sides and their interrelations, thereby forming his judgements, making up his mind and working out his plans. Such is the complete process of knowing a situation which a military man goes through before he formulates a strategic plan, a campaign plan or a battle.

"Problems of Strategy in China's Revolutionary War" (December 1936) Selected Works Vol. I, p. 188 LRB 235.

The Creativity Process

You cannot sit in your ivory tower and run the company—unless you are a one-man operation. You are extremely dependent on the resources that you have around you—basically your staff, and as you can see on the preceeding pages Mao put a lot of emphasis on involving superiors, peers and subordinates in situation analysis, decision making, implementation etc. He points out that as the head of an organization you cannot expect to know everything yourself, nor to do everything and as you move up the ladder and your company becomes larger and larger, the ability to work through others become more and more vital. I come back to this later in the book, but I want to emphasize this up front and also describe some methods that you should use to get as much as possible out of your people when you interact with them in meetings.

I also want to stress at this point that involving employees at all levels is very beneficial when you are solving problems. It is also very motivating for your people and will help you obtain their loyalty and support. My experience is that there is a lot of energy in your employees irrespective of where they work in the organization. The trick is to tap that energy through involvement and respect. I have numerous examples of strong contributions from my staff in matters that I hardly believed that they were interested in.

Creativity is something that is very important when you manage your company. The top manager, his management team and all the employees in the company are faced all the time with problems that they have to find a solution to. In the pursuit of these solutions creativity is an important factor. A short and simple definition of creativity could be the ability to find new combinations and to be innovative. We can divide the creative process into four steps:

- **Preparation**
  Although many would say that you couldn't prepare for the creation of a good idea, the fact is that all good ideas and innovative solutions come after meticulous and systematic preparation—consciously or unconsciously. This preparation can then result in a spontaneous creation. The content of the preparation could be to

  i. define the problem
  ii. limit the problem

   iii. obtain material and facts

   iv. analyze the material and facts

- **Incubation**

  It is not normal for good solutions to be found immediately after the preparation phase. However, the conclusions are being handled subconsciously and it can take a long time before the ideas are created—i.e from a few minutes to years.

- **Solution**

  The objective of all creative activity is the moment in which the new idea comes to fruition. This moment gives the creator a high degree of satisfaction. This moment can occur

     i. when it is most unexpected

     ii. after a long period of iterations between preparation and incubation

     iii. during periods of relaxation and rest. Remember that Archimedes discovered his physical laws in the bathtub

     iv. after the solution or the idea is on the table, the innovator feels the need to communicate his ideas to the world

- **Verification**

  This is a part of the process where

     i. one seeks confirmation of the fact that one has a correct solution

     ii. the idea or solution is refined

     iii. many good ideas do not come to fruition because creative people are so preoccupied with new ideas that they have no time to complete the previous ideas.

     iv. during the verification process, new problems may occur and we may be forced to repeat the creative process several times.

If I look back at the way this book came about, it followed these steps. Although it took years to get it completed in the present form,

I went through Preparation, Incubation, Solution and Verification, as I have done in many other situations.

Creative people often have the following personality traits:

- They are **flexible** and **openminded**
- They are **observant**—they recognize far more details around them than the normal human being
- They are **motivated**—they are restless and interested in new things that happen around them

In a creative environment there are alternate career opportunities, superiors recognize the good work (and for that matter not-so-good), ideas are being used, there is a lot of freedom in the way work can be done and there are many training opportunities for employees. In the previous frame you will see quotations from Chairman Mao that describes practices that are supportive of creative environments.

Methods to Improve Your Creativity

Develop your own methods for being creative and efficient. Stay loyal to these and develop them as you go along and get more experience. The following are two methods that I have used more than a hundred times and I am pretty certain that they are very efficient compared to unsystematic approaches that many apply. What I do with these techniques is to "pick the brains" of my associates and myself by asking questions, making associations and involving staff at all levels of the organization.

- **Brainstorming**

One simple method that I recommend that you learn and apply as often as possible is brainstorming. The purpose of brainstorming is to create as many ideas or viewpoints as possible.

i. Set the scene
    ➢ Gather a group of people—your own employees or others—who have knowledge about the subject

> Help them to prepare themselves by giving advance notice about the meeting, the purpose, the subject and the problems
> Define the subject clearly
> Have a flipchart easel available
> Have felt pens of different colors available

ii. Focus on one subject at a time
iii. Run the process as follows

> Ask questions
> Jot down all the ideas on the flipchart
> Remember all the time the 4 ground rules for creativity (preparation, incubation, solution and verification) and focus on where in the creative process you are at any time
> Post the flipcharts on the wall—then all members of the group have a common reference
> Monitor the time

  ❖ Maximize the number of ideas within a predetermined time period
  ❖ Work until you have a certain number of ideas on the flipcharts

> Encourage people to develop different views and constructively challenge the current paradigms
> Spur ideas by

  ❖ Enlarging
  ❖ Diminishing
  ❖ Replacing
  ❖ Changing the order
  ❖ Doing the opposite
  ❖ Combining
  ❖ Asking if there are other areas for use
  ❖ Refining
  ❖ Modifying

➢ Document and edit the results and send them to the participants

➢ Refine the ideas and use them as the basis for the more thorough work that is required to complete the problem solving

➢ Use the documentation next time you convene a meeting with the same subject

With some training you will find that this is a very productive way of solving problems and stimulating the creative process. Furthermore, it involves your staff, which is very motivating. You learn to know them and you release a lot of the energy that that they have.

I recently heard about a company that needed to transport water from Europe to Asia. They thought thoroughly for a long time to find an appropriate solution. They started to look for analogies. Suddenly a wise guy thought: "Why not use the bag-in-box concept that is used in the wine industry"—i.e. put a plastic bag with wine inside a cardboard box. His idea was to manufacture a big bag to be put inside a standard container and fill this bag with water. Then it would be put on board a ship or a railway-carriage and transported to its destination.

- **Mindmapping**

Another way of "picking the brains" of a group of people and even yourself is to use a method that is called mindmapping.

Through this process you will be able to identify important parts of a subject through associations that are made during the process that is described on the following page. Let me give you an example. We are going to make a presentation of the United States.

i. The box with a thick line and a black field to the left tells what the main subject is.

ii. The rectangular boxes describe what our main headlines in the speech are, i.e.

- ➢ Geography
- ➢ History
- ➢ Population
- ➢ Economy
- ➢ Great personalities

iii. The round boxes indicate what we will be handling under each of the main history subjects . . .

iv. The rectangular boxes with rounded corners are details related to each of the main history subjects.

- ➢ The First Settlers
- ➢ The American Revolution
- ➢ The Wars (where the sub-subjects are indicated in green circles).

Mindmapping

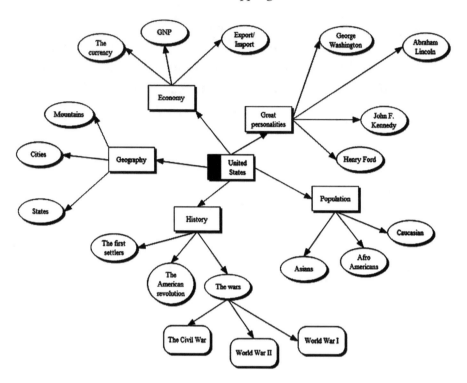

For most of us, however, this chart is not very practical. Ideally, we would like an outline where you get all these points after each other in the sequence that you desire. One thing that you can do is to take the charts on the preceding page and convert it to an outline. There is a tool for this that I strongly recommend. Its name is Inspiration. Inspiration is a computer program that helps you do the mindmapping exercise and then has a function that converts the chart into an outline with just a mouse click. If you want to edit the outline you can do that very easily by "click and drag" functions. As you can see on the adjacent page, the outline on the left hand side is not exactly the same as on the right. To make this was extremely easy and did not even involve "copy and paste functions". If you want to make comments in a narrative form you can do that very easily as well. In addition there are numerous other circumstances in the work situation where it is beneficial to work with brain-mapping.

To get more information about the program, visit Inspiration's website—*www.inspiration.com.*

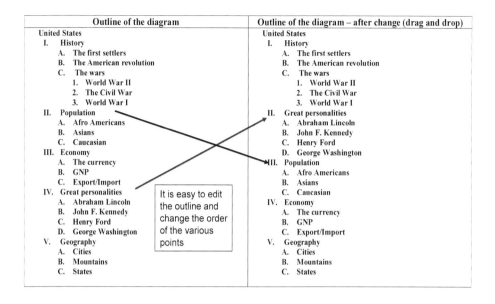

Outline of the diagram	Outline of the diagram – after change (drag and drop)

United States
I.   History
    A. The first settlers
    B. The American revolution
    C. The wars
      1. World War II
      2. The Civil War
      3. World War I
II. Population
    A. Afro Americans
    B. Asians
    C. Caucasian
III. Economy
    A. The currency
    B. GNP
    C. Export/Import
IV. Great personalities
    A. Abraham Lincoln
    B. John F. Kennedy
    C. Henry Ford
    D. George Washington
V. Geography
    A. Cities
    B. Mountains
    C. States
 	
It is easy to edit the outline and change the order of the various points
	United States
	I. History
	    A. The first settlers
	    B. The American revolution
	    C. The wars
	      1. World War II
	      2. The Civil War
	      3. World War I
	II. Great personalities
	    A. Abraham Lincoln
	    B. John F. Kennedy
	    C. Henry Ford
	    D. George Washington
	III. Population
	    A. Afro Americans
	    B. Asians
	    C. Caucasian
	IV. Economy
	    A. The currency
	    B. GNP
	    C. Export/Import
	V. Geography
	    A. Cities
	    B. Mountains
	    C. States

To be a creative and innovative person it is important to have information. I therefore suggest that you adapt a style that is inquisitive, where you are curious and seek information and knowledge. Without being rude or conceited, challenge viewpoints, traditions, rules etc.

Read everything that has the potential to give you knowledge of the background that is needed in different contexts. I am thinking of books—trade literature as well as novels—that tell about people and their lives in your own culture and in other parts of the world. Read newspapers—first of course local business dailies, but also international newspapers like *Financial Times, International Herald Tribune* etc. Instead of buying paper copies you can subscribe to the closed net-pages of those newspapers you are interested in or look at their open pages that do not cost anything. I also recommend that you read international magazines like *Newsweek, Time, Fortune, Harvard Business Review* etc. They are full of articles that any businesswoman or -man should have as background in a competitive world where things are constantly changing. Read also airline in-flight magazines—it is amazing how many interesting and relevant feature articles that are found in them.

The internet is also a tremendous source of information. To be able to find the information that you are after, learn how to use search engines like Google, Yahoo and others. In addition, read the web-sites of companies and institutions that are relevant for you.

If you would like to subscribe to articles that are of special interest to you, www.highbeam.com is a useful address.

A source of information that I find very useful, are annual reports of various companies. These are a very good source for learning about general matters and specifics such as strategies, values, mission and vision of the company in question. In addition, thorough scrutiny provides you with information about a certain industry, its competitive activities, names of key persons that you could network with and many other things that can be of value to you.

Retain information that you get on your computer. Things that you read on the net, you can easily copy and put into a text-processing file (like MS Word). With a scanner (often low-cost) you can scan in newspaper articles and excerpts from books and keep them in your text-processing system.

In general, reading or seeking information provides you with a background that makes it possible for you to generate ideas in many areas.

Your Company's Route to Success—Overview

What Did Mao Say?

The only way to settle questions of an ideological nature or controversial issues among the people is by the democratic method, the method of discussion, of criticism, of persuasion and education, and not by the method of coercion or repression.

"On the Correct Handling og Contradictions Among the People"
(February 27, 1957), 1st pocket ed., p. 11. LRB 52.

The educational policy of the college is to cultivate a firm and correct political orientation, an industrious and simple style of work, and flexible strategy and tactics. These are three essentials in the making of a . . . . revolutionary soldier. It is in accordance with these essentials that the staff teaches and students study.

"To be Attacked by the Enemy is not A Bad Thing, but a Good Thing".
(May 26, 1939). 1st pocket ed., p. 3. LRB 146.

Diligence and frugality should be practiced in running factories and shops and all state-owned, co-operative and other enterprises. The principle of diligence and frugality should be observed in everything. This principle of economy is one of the basic principles of socialist economics. China is a big country, but she is still very poor. It will take several decades to make China prosperous. Even then we will still have to observe the principle of diligence and frugality. But it is in the coming few decades, during the present series of five-year-plans, that we must particularly advocate diligence and frugality, that we must pay special attention to economy.

Introductory note to "Running a Co-operative diligently and frugally"
(1955), The Socialist Upsurge in China's Countryside,
Chinese ed, Vol. I. LRB 187.

Wherever we happen to be, we must treasure our manpower and material resources, and must not take a short view and indulge in wastefulness and extravagance. Wherever we are from the very first year of our work we must bear in mind the many years to come, the protracted war that must be maintained, the counter-offensive, and the work of reconstruction after the enemy's expulsion. On the one hand, never be wasteful and extravagant; on the other, actively expand production. Previously, in some places people suffered a great deal because they did not take the long view and neglected economy in manpower and expansion of production. The lesson is there and attention must be called to it.

"We Must Learn to Do Economic Work" (January 10, 1945),
Selected Works, Vol III, p.244. LRB 187.

It (a regional or sub-regional bureau of the Central Committee of the Party) should constantly have a grip on the progress of the work, exchange experience and correct mistakes; it should not wait several months, half a year or a year before holding summing-up meetings for a general check-up and a general correction of mistakes. Waiting leads to great loss, while correcting mistakes as soon as they occur reduces loss.

"On the Policy Concerning Industry and Committee" (February 27, 1948)
Selected Works, Vol. IV, p. 204. LRB 228.

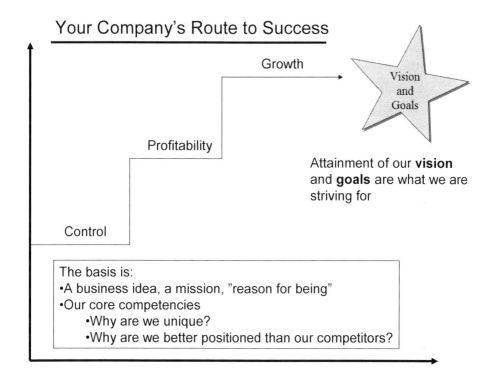

What I want to do is to guide you from the situation that you have today which might not be in accordance with the ideas that you have for the company. This is a situation that you can be in whether you

o   are running a company that has been in operation for years or
o   you are responsible for a company that is in the process of being started up

Both these situations require that you do things in a systematic and orderly fashion and my objective is to show you how to do this irrespective of the situation that you are in. When we proceed you might feel that this is pretty basic and that many of the things that I am pointing at are in place. However, in my experience, many of the companies that enjoy the admiration of surroundings and society, have serious flaws if you audit their operations. Therefore, I strongly believe that my text to a large extent will be helpful for most companies.

On the preceeding page I show a simple graph where the X-axis shows the time and the Y shows the development in the type of objectives that you have. Examples here could be Volumes (how many units do you want to produce, sell, transport etc.), Revenue, Profit etc. that you want to attain. However, what the axis also could represent is a more abstract description of where you want to be in the future.

In my experience there are three very important stages in a company's long-term development—the first is **Control**, the second is **Profitability** and the third is **Growth**. And I stress—in this order. Many business failures have been caused by the fact that the owners wanted quick growth without understanding that in order to do that control and profitability are important parts of the fundament that all companies stand on. Business leaders that I have stressed this to in board meetings, during seminars, personal conversations etc. have come to me years after and said: "Lars, I should have listened to you when you stressed the importance of Control, Profitability and then Growth" or said "thank you for this excellent piece of advice". I picked up this important principle when I worked for Citibank. I am convinced that this management principle has been an extremely good reason for their success. Furthermore, I am convinced that the reason why they are tackling problems in a superb way and probably have avoided lots of failures is that they have done things with a pace that takes this into account.

My experience is that if you (the management) do not have control over your operations you will constantly look over your shoulder and focus on matters that definitely are not paving your way for the future. In reality this means that you have to respond to nasty audit reports, you are running out of liquidity, your board is bothering you with questions, you have to have endless discussions with your bank to get help to deal with a difficult cash-flow, just to mention a few of the things that bad control can cause. In most countries bad control also can move you into a situation where you are violating laws and regulations.

Control comprises quite a lot. Irrespective of how market-oriented and extrovert you are—mind my words—make Control a word of honor and do not consider it as bureaucracy and red tape. Support your control resources (internal auditors, accountants, controller, legal department etc.). If they have authority in your organization you will avoid a lot of problems. Respect their standpoints and put your foot down when f. ex. your top salesman wants to cut corners in obtaining an important order that could give you glory in the short run, but might cause severe problems in the longer perspective—to give you a general example, of which I have seen a great number.

Profitability is the aim of all corporate endeavors. It is one—but the most important—of many objectives that a company has. If there is no profit, the company is bound to go under sooner or later. With no profit a company has no means of prospering and developing itself. Furthermore, if there is no profit, there is no incentive for the owners to invest in the company.

Through profit the company creates value for its owners, its employees and its customers. Profit—normally—means tax income for society, development and job security for the employees, better products and higher product quality for its customers.

How do we express profit? A simple definition is that it is the income minus all costs associated with the income. Profitability is the profit measured against income, total capital, equity etc., normally expressed as a percentage, a ratio or similar. Later in the book we will examine closer how one should measure profitability.

Very often when a company is in a situation with squeezed profit, management is obliged to do something. However, there is frequently a reluctance to take proper action because they believe (often wishfully) that there arc sunnier days ahead, they want to be considerate of the employees, it might create bad press, they might lose key employees because they feel that their jobs are in jeopardy etc. It is very important to be realistic and not let a need for action drag on too long without doing anything. Change has to be made in time in order to maintain the solidity of the company. Very often the dilemma is to sacrifice some jobs today to save the company rather than doing nothing and risk that the company goes bust or reduces it's future chances for success. Remember the following quote: *Place the problems on the table. This should be done not only by the "squad leader", but by the committee members too . . . . Whenever problems arise, place the problem on the table for discussion, take some decisions and the problems will be solved. If problems exist and are not put on the table, they will remain unsolved for a long time and even drag on for years. The "squad leader" and the committee members should show understanding in their relations with each other. Nothing is more important than mutual understanding, support and friendship between the secretary and the committee members, between the Central Committee and its regional bureaus and between the regional bureaus and the Party Committees*

Therefore, it is extremely important that this is well understood by all stakeholders and that management understands their role in creating the necessary change to bring the company back on track again.

Growth is as common an objective for a corporation as profitability. We want to increase the revenue and the profit, we want to explore new markets, we want to sell more to existing customers, we want to increase production factors like employees and assets like machines, buildings etc. I am extremely supportive of efforts to grow beyond today's size. However, costs increase when you make a leap in your capacity like opening up a branch in a new city or country. When you build a new building, buy a new machine, or hire new employees your cost level is escalated—very often a long time before you get the associated revenue. For these and many other good reasons it is extremely important that you have management control over your current activities, that you have management capacity to handle the extensions that you are planning and that you have sufficient profit from the daily operations or accumulated reserves and through that the financial solidity that is needed to endure a situation that is not completely up to the assumptions that you used to support your decision.

Apply this acid test when you are in an extension situation. What is the picture if:

o   the time we assume will be three times longer than expected
o   the revenue will be one third of what we had expected and
o   the costs associated with the project will be three times higher than planned

If your calculations still are positive you can go ahead with a lot more likelihood of being successful. This is of course an exaggeration, but there is a lot of sense in this approach.

What I want to get over to you by this gloomy picture is that you need to be realistic whenever you are in an investment situation. I am certain that many seasoned managers strongly agree with my description.

Control, **Profitability** and **Growth** are the basis for the book and I will come back to them thoroughly later and focus on what they comprise in practical terms.

III

The Ideological Platform for Your Company

What Did Mao Say?

An army without a culture is a dull-witted army, and a dull-witted army cannot defeat the enemy.

"The United Front in Cultural Work" (October 30, 1944),
Selected Works, Vol III, p. 235. LRB 303.

For a military school, the most important question is the selection of a director and instructors and the adoption of an educational policy.

"Problems of Strategy in China's Revolutionary War (December 1936)
Selected Works, Vol. I, p. 185. LRB 166.

Our troops must observe the correct principles that govern the relationship between the army and the people, between the army and the Party, between the officers and the men, and between military work and political work, and relations among the cadres, and must never commit the errors of warlordism. Officers must cherish their men and must not be indifferent to their well-being or resort to corporal punishment, the army must cherish the people and never encroach upon their interest, the army must respect the government and the Party and never "assert independence".

"Get Organized" (November 29, 1943)
Selected Works, Vol. III pp.158-59. LRB 138.

The educational policy of the college is to cultivate a firm and correct political orientation, an industrious and simple style of work, and flexible strategy and tactics. These are three essentials in the making of an anti-Japanese revolutionary soldier. It is in accordance with these essentials that the staff teaches and students study.

To be Attacked by the Enemy is not A Bad Thing, but a Good Thing. (May 26, 1939) 1st pocket ed., p. 3. LRB 146.

Our Army has always two policies. First, we must be ruthless to our enemies; we must overpower and annihilate them. Second, we must be kind to our own, to the people, to our comrades and to our superiors and subordinates, and unite with them.

Party for Model study delegates from the Rear Army Detachments (September 18, 1944) Speech at the reception given by the Central Committee of the Party for model study delegates from the Rear Army Detachments (September 18, 1944). LRB 148.

We must know how to take good care of the cadres. There are several ways of doing so.

First, give them guidance. This means allowing them a free hand in their work so that they have the courage to assume responsibility and, at the same time giving them timely instructions so that, guided by the party's political line, they are able to make full use of their initiative.

Second, raise their level. This mans educating them by giving them the opportunity to study so that they can enhance their theoretical understanding and their working ability.

Third, check up on their work, and help them sum up their experience, carry forward their achievements and correct their mistakes. To assign work without checking up and to take notice only when serious mistakes are made—that is not the way to take care of cadres.

Fourth, in general use the method of persuasion with cadres who have made mistakes, and help them to correct their mistakes. The method of struggle should be confined to those who make serious mistakes and nevertheless refuse to accept the guidance. Here patience is essential. It is wrong lightly to label people "opportunists" or lightly to begin "waging" struggle against them.

Fifth, *help them with their difficulties. When cadres are in difficulty as a result of illness, straitened means, or domestic or other trouble, we must be sure to give them as much care as possible.*

This is to take good care of cadres.

"The Role of the Chinese Communist Party in the National War" (October 1938), Selected Works, Vol. II. p. 203. LRB 283.

It is very important that the owners, the board and the management of the company have shared perceptions of what the **Mission**, the **Vision** and the **Values** and **Culture** of the company are. As the head of the organization or part of the management group you must recognize the benefit of communicating a clear and compelling statement of future direction to all your employees. A description of the road ahead and how the organization defines success and what the important shared values and beliefs are, can have a powerful and positive impact on the organization. There are many schools of thought regarding this and often there is not a clear distinction between mission, vision and values. This you will see from the examples that I cite below. In the following I will describe them separately and try to demonstrate that they are different. I also believe that there is a logical order between them. First comes the Mission, thereafter the Vision and then the Values. Later—in order to position the company and create operational focus—we will determine what the Core Competencies are. However, corporations and scholars define this differently.

The Ideological Platform for a Company

What business are we in?

Core Competencies
What are our comparable advantages – our
particular reasons for success?

Mission Statement
What is our reason for being?

Vision
What do we want to achieve and look like down the road – in 5 years?

What are our Corporate Values?

What is our Corporate Culture?

What are our Policies

Mission

This chapter is inspired by David L. Calfee's article "Get your Mission Statement Working" that appeared in *Management Review*/January 1993.

The Mission is a description of the companies' reason for being. It states what it is that we should be for whom. Very often you see that mission statements are very introvertly expressed, while I think it is important to make an extrovert statement where we define who our clients are and what we are doing for them.

There are a variety of ways to define a company mission:

o Some companies have elected to describe at length what success will look like, how it will be measured and how competitive advantages will be created and maintained.

o Others have boiled their mission statement down to a single phrase like NOKIA, whose mission statement is "Connecting People".

A mission statement should enthuse an organization by describing exciting future possibilities in which all can share. And it should signal the critical skill and as Mr. Calfee's article points out: "*A mission statement should be more than words on a piece of paper. It should be a living, breathing document of your organization. A mission statement should provide focus for the organization, to get everybody pulling in the same direction in pursuit of common and well-understood goals. It should energize the capabilities that, once built, can serve as the foundation for marketplace success*".

Mr. Calfee stresses the following: "*Don't just frame your mission statement and hang it on the wall; make sure that all employees in your organization know how their work fits in with the corporation's overall goals*".

A mission statement is also an important tool when you communicate with the external world. Stakeholders like customers, banks, potential employees, suppliers, the press, governmental bodies and so forth get an opinion of your company when you communicate your mission statement.

When you create your mission statement—the following recommendations from Mr. Calfee will help you to make it operational.

o   Craft a statement that answers three basic questions:

- What business will we be in down the road?
- What are our objectives?
- How will we win?

o   Communicate the mission statement throughout the organization
o   Translate the key elements of the statement into relevant performance objectives to employees at all levels."

Some other requirements for a mission statement are described by Karl Albrecht in his book "The Northbound Train". To be useful a mission statement must have three components:

o   It should be focused
o   It should have a sense of noble purpose of signalling that you are doing something that is really worth doing
o   It should have a plausible chance of success

When you work on a mission statement you should highlight the most important words and describe what the meaning of them is. This is particularly important

o   from a quality assurance point of view
o   from an educational point of view

Let's look at some examples of mission statements (not necessarily the latest):

JPMorganChase—Financial Services:

We create exceptional value by integrating our deep and broad global capabilities:

- ➤ *Integrity—Set the standard*
- ➤ *Clients—Build relationships that they value*
- ➤ *Excellence—In our people and what we deliver*

➤ *Leadership—In everything we do*
➤ *Diversity—Stronger because of it*
➤ *Teamwork—Deliver the Global Network*
➤ *Quality—Get it right the first time*
➤ *Initiative—Find a way*

Amgen—Pharmaceuticals:

➤ *Amgen Values*

   o *Be science based*
   o *Work in teams*
   o *Compete intensely and win*
   o *Create value for patients, staff and stockholders*
   o *Trust and respect for each other*
   o *Collaborate, communicate, and build consensus*
   o *Ensure quality*
   o *Be ethical*

General Electric's—Industrial Conglomerate

The following is a good description of this gigantic company's phrasing for their values as they were described on their web-pages:

For more than 125 years, GE has been admired for its performance and imaginative spirit. The businesses that we invent and build fuel the global economy and improve people's lives.

Today, we are 11 technology, services and financial businesses with more than 300,000 employees in 160 countries around the world.

What unifies us? Our Actions and Values.

What we do and how we work is distinctly GE. It's a way of thinking and working that has grounded our performance for decades. It's a way of talking about our work and ourselves that takes the best from our past and expresses it in the spirit and language of GE today.

It's about who we are, what we believe, where we're headed, how we'll get there. It's how we imagine, solve, build and lead.

Imagine

From the very beginnings of our company, when Thomas Edison was changing the world with the power of ideas, GE has always stood for one capability above all others—the ability to imagine.

Imagine is a sense of possibility that allows for a freedom beyond mere invention. Imagine dares to be something greater.

At GE, Imagine is an invitation to dream and do things that you didn't know you could do.

Because at GE the act of imagining is fused with empowerment—the confidence that what we imagine, we can make happen.

Solve

Every business has to have a reason to exist—a reason that answers the fundamental question of "why are we here?"

For GE, the big question has a simple answer: We exist to solve problems—for our customers, our communities and societies, and for ourselves.

Build

From 0 to 60 in six seconds? Try zero to $5 billion in five years.

It's not so much a vision for our future—where we're headed is in many ways a reflection of where we've already been. It's not a destination. It's a quest. A quest for growth. And when we look to the future, we know that for us, there's only one way to get there. Build.

Lead

Imagine. Solve. Build. Each of these is merely a word without one vital element. Lead.

GE is already synonymous with leadership. But with this mantle comes responsibility. And it's not just a responsibility to maintain the status quo or manage what worked yesterday. It's the bigger responsibility to change.

Because change is the essence of what it means to lead.

It's a call to action that engages our unceasing curiosity, our passion, and our drive to be first in everything that we do.

We Are a Company to Believe In.

In the end, our success is measured not only by our ability to think big, dazzling thoughts, but by our commitment to sweat the small stuff that brings ideas to life. It's a way—thinking and doing—that has been at the heart of GE for years.

The worth of this framework is how we translate it into our own personal work ethic and then extend it to our teams, businesses, cultures and different regions of the world. It's permission to cast aside any approach that seems dated—to imagine, solve, build and lead a better way of doing things.

Values

While GE has always performed with integrity and values, each business generation expresses those values according to the circumstances of the times. Now more than ever the expression and adherence to values is vital.

More than just a set of words, these values embody the spirit of GE at its best. They reflect the energy and spirit of a company that has the solid foundation to lead change as business evolves. And they articulate a code of behavior that guides us through that change with integrity.

The words reflected here represent a revitalization of our values. They are a call to action that asks every GE employee to recommit to a common set of beliefs about how we work in our world today. And while some of these words are new in their expression, they are based on a continuum of how GE has grown and performed through generations.

They are our words and our values . . . in our own voice.

Passionate
Curious
Resourceful
Accountable
Teamwork
Committed
Open
Energizing

Always With Unyielding Integrity

McDonald's—Fast Food

Their people Vision—*defines what they strive towards as an employer. Simply, they aspire* . . . .

. . . . *"To Be the Best Employer in Each Community Around the World".*

Their People Promise—*We want the more than people around the world who work at McDonald's in 119 countries, and all future employees, to know that:*

We value You, Your Growth and Your Contributions.

Their commitment to their employees—*their Five People Principles are:*

1. **Respect and Recognition**

   Managers treat employees as they want to be treated they respect and value the employees and recognize them formally for good work performance, extra effort, teamwork and customer service.

2. **Values and Leadership Behavior**

   - *All of us act in the best interest of the company*
   - *We communicate openly, listening for understanding and valuing diverse opinions*
   - *We accept personal accountability*
   - *We coach to learn them*

3. **Competitive Pay and Benefits**

   - *Pay is at or above local market*
   - *Employees value their pay and benefits*

4. Learning, Development and Personal Growth

- *Employees receive work experience that teaches skills and values that last a lifetime*
- *Employees are provided with the tools they need to develop personally and professionally*

5. Resources to Get the Job Done

- *Employees have the resources they need to serve the customer*
- *Restaurants are adequately staffed to allow for a good customer experience as well as to provide schedule flexibility, work-life balance and time for training.*

These are very altruistic statements and reflect the importance that McDonald's puts on people. They are their most important assets. Their employees are meeting millions of customers (guests) every day and these customers perceive McDonald's by the McDonald's employees' service attitude and execution—in addition, of course, by the food quality. They generate millions of small transactions every day and give millions of customers "their moment of truth" at the same time.

"Moments of truth" are all the small occasions when we meet our customers every day. This could be in the purchase situation, during a presentation, during delivery, when they utilize our product, when they receive an invoice, when they call our service center to make an inquiry, when they hit our websites, when they read about us in the newspapers, when representatives of the company appear on TV, on the radio etc. During these occasions we must make a positive, lasting impression—with the aim of getting prospective customers as customers or to make certain that existing customers remain customers who believe in what we are doing.

American Airlines—Air Transportation

At American Airlines we work hard to make sure that your travel experience is something special.

Medtronic—Medical Equipment

I will spend a few pages on Medtronic because they—in my mind—use the mission in the way that it should be used in order to vitalize and energize. This is the way that they express their mission:

Our mission is to contribute to human welfare through

1. *Focused growth*
2. *Unsurpassed quality*
3. *Fair profit*
4. *Personal worth of employees*
5. *Good citizenship*

The significant thing about the Medtronic mission statement is that not one word has been changed since it was originally written in 1960. At that time the young company was trying to introduce an implantable pacemaker. Sales were rising rapidly but so were expenses. The cash was going out faster than it was coming in. The company was broke and the following actions were taken:

Earl, the company president visited local bankers in Minneapolis to set up a line of credit. All of them slammed the door in his face. He commissioned a market research study to demonstrate the potential for the pacemaker, and it predicted that the maximum number of devices to be implanted through all history was less than 10,000! No money there.

One board member suggested to Earl that they were lacking a statement of purpose. So Earl sat down and wrote this mission statement, not one word of which has changed over the (first) years. The president took the mission statement to a local venture capitalist and made his case. He got his funding by giving up the bulk of his equity in the company, but the company survived and grew to the significant market value it has today. Over the years the mission statement has changed and today it reads as follows:

- *To contribute to human welfare by application of biomedical engineering in the research, design, manufacture, and sale of instruments or appliances that alleviate pain, restore health, and extend life.*

- *To direct our growth in the areas of biomedical engineering where we display maximum strength and ability; to gather people and facilities that tend to augment these areas; to continuously build on these areas through education and knowledge assimilation; to avoid participation in areas where we cannot make unique and worthy contributions.*
- *To strive without reserve for the greatest possible reliability and quality in our products; to be the unsurpassed standard of comparison and to be recognized as a company of dedication, honesty, integrity, and service.*
- *To make a fair profit on current operations to meet our obligations, sustain our growth, and reach our goals.*
- *To recognize the personal worth of employees by providing an employment framework that allows personal satisfaction in work accomplished, security, advancement opportunity, and means to share in the company's success.*
- *To maintain good citizenship as a company.*

I strongly recommend that you create a structured process around your efforts to create a mission, state your values and decide on your own company's vision. Study the visions and missions of well-known and not so well-known companies by looking at their web sites, annual reports and other material. This will certainly give you inspiration as to the formulation of these things in your own company.

The way Medtronic is reinforcing the content and the spirit of their mission statement is in my mind an example of how it should be done to make the statement more than a set of words. Through their focus in many contexts the statement becomes a living document in the organization—well known and creating credibility among the stakeholders i.e. the shareholders, the employees, the customers, the suppliers, their bank etc.

Moments of truth are—as we stressed above—all the small occasions where we every day meet our customers. This applies to

- JPMorganChase
- Amgen
- General Electric
- McDonald's
- American Airlines

- **Medtronic**

and all other companies in the world. Whenever they meet a customer an impression will be made that will be decisive for the continued relations with that customer. Remember—"You seldom get a second chance to make a first impression". Therefore it is important to do it right the first time.

Vision

The purpose of the vision is to put up a leading star—a direction in which we are going. It is very important to visualize the vision. You must preach the vision all the time and continually reaffirm it.

As Tom Peters says: *"Effective visions are inspiring. They are clear and challenging—and about excellence. They make sense and can stand the test of time, they are stable, yet flexible. An effective vision empowers people and prepares for the future while having roots in the past.*

In line with the logic that I described earlier I will define the Vision as the long term objectives that we want to attain.

According to Donald T. Phillips's book "Lincoln on Leadership", Peters and Austin wrote the following: *"You have to know where you're going. To be able to state it clearly and concisely. And you have to care about it passionately. That all adds up to a vision. The concise statement or picture of where the company and its people are heading and why they should be proud of it."*

As you can see from the above there are many ways of expressing company Missions, Visions and Values. However, there are five themes that seem to be addressed in a majority of them. These themes are Customers, Employees, Excellence, Quality and Ethics.

When you craft these sentences and words you therefore must

o   be **Customer** oriented,
o   recognize that your **Employees** are among your most important assets,
o   understand that **Excellence** is a must to survive,
o   be obsessed by the pursuit of **Quality,**
o   be **Ethical** in all your dealings.

Corporate Values

Corporate Values or Basic Beliefs as they f.ex. were called at IBM, state principles of a higher order that the corporation intends to follow in their dealings. It is very useful to have such principles or beliefs stated. It makes life easier and they give the employees something to hold on to when it's storming around them in a competitive situation, when they have to handle difficult personnel situations, are negotiating with suppliers etc. These basic beliefs lived well for close to a hundred years. In the beginning of this century it was decided to revamp the values and it is interesting to note the following about IBM's process to establish values after having been a successful company in its markets. The quote is from their web-site:

Corporate values

During four days of July 2003, IBM employees around the world engaged in an online intranet discussion called 'ValuesJam' to shape and define the values that should guide the company and its people in the years ahead. Thousands of postings and emails were thoroughly analysed and distilled into three values shared by all at IBM.

- *Dedication to every client's success*
- *Innovation that matters—for our company and for the world*
- *Trust and personal responsibility in all relationships*

A dedication to client or customer success is not a new concept in IBM. Our tradition of superior customer service is legendary. It was one of the three 'Basic Beliefs' held by IBMers in the last century (the others being 'respect for the individual' and 'the pursuit of excellence').

Core Competencies

After recognition of what our mission is we should spend time on defining what our core competencies are. Core competencies are things that make us unique compared to our competitors and that enhance the likelihood of success in reaching our vision. Core competencies can include the following factors:

o   Competence in areas like

   o   Technical skills
   o   Market understanding
   o   Administrative efficiency
   o   Production management

o   Innovative capabilities—particular reserves of individuals with the ability to bring out new products
o   Location

   o   Close to market
   o   Close to raw materials
   o   Close to skilled manpower supply

o   Financial Strength and solidity because of high equity ratio and/or cash position, and/or solid cash generated by the operations
o   Availability of foreign financing if that is required because we enjoy credibility and confidence in the financial markets and among investors
o   Right owners—i.e. owners that have a strategic or industrial perspective on the activity and not only a short-term profit requirement
o   Enthusiastic and supportive staff that stands by you on good and bad days.
o   Skilled and competent work force with an ability to execute and a good labor market in case you need to expand
o   Goodwill among government/authorities/trade associations/politicians
o   Patents that ensure that your intellectual property (IPR) is protected or that your proprietary information is protected in other ways.

o   Not doing harm to the environment because we have appropriate policies, a good attitude among employees, monitoring systems etc.
o   Strategic partnerships that will be beneficial for product development, production, marketing, distribution etc.
o   Flexibility to change, to modify, to build up and build down personnel, equipment, facilities, markets etc.
o   Cost benefits due to low cost labor, efficient machinery and equipment etc.

Identify your core competencies together with your staff, your management team, your board, outside resources and others. Be honest and critical so that you do not put anything on this important list that really does not deserve it.

This exercise may also be useful when you want to identify the core competencies that you do not have but that could be desirable to have. As a consequence you might have to initiate actions to acquire such competencies.

Policies

It is important to have policies and guidelines that can act as a guide for management and other stakeholders in carrying out their responsibility. I am stressing this because there are frequent instances of inappropriate attitudes and actions where people do things that either are illegal or bad behaviour. However, often wrongdoing happens because there are no rules that explain what is right and what is wrong and what is desired behaviour under different circumstances.

In the business world, changes happen every day, every hour, every minute. Businesses continually evolve to keep up with the demands of a changing market place, economy and society. Every day your company will be challenged to meet these demands and to ensure that your company maintains the position that you have as goal. You and your associates should meet these challenges in a consistent way. You should set policies and create procedures for corporate issues that are vital to your success.

Most companies understand the value of their staff and have policies to create an environment that is conducive to attracting, developing and retaining competent employees irrespective of gender, age, race, marital status, education, religion etc. The reasons for this are partially legal requirements. However, I am certain that many companies, in addition to an altruistic attitude, also understand that consideration and empathy lead to a maximum effort from their employees and the best results. Consequently their policies often start with a focus on people.

However, companies have many other focuses for policies such as organization, values, legal matters, emergencies and crises, public affairs, conflicts of interest, accounting practices, presence in foreign cultures and international operations, environmental matters, health and safety etc.

As a guideline for the employees in their dealings with their colleagues, customers and suppliers, the authorities and others—many companies have adapted codes of conduct that provide a framework for the employees to understand values and ethical standards. They are normally very determined that their employees are conversant with these codes and spend time and resources on seminars and courses to reinforce them for their employees and particularly for those that have jobs where they deal with the external environment and society.

The following is an example of one of the policies that International Business Machines (IBM) has established. The source for this is information is the internet and the subject is their Environmental affairs policy:

"IBM is committed to environmental affairs leadership in all of its business activities. IBM has had long-standing corporate policies of providing a safe and healthful work place, protecting the environment, and conserving energy and natural resources, which were formalized in 1967, 1971 and 1974 respectively. They have served the environment and our business well over the years and provide the foundation for the following corporate policy objectives:

- *Provide a safe and healthful workplace and ensure that personnel are properly trained and have appropriate safety and emergency equipment.*
- *Be an environmentally responsible neighbor in the communities where we operate, and act promptly and responsibly to correct incidents or conditions that endanger health, safety, or the environment. Report them to authorities promptly and inform affected parties as appropriate.*
- *Conserve natural resources by reusing and recycling materials, purchasing recycled materials, and using recyclable packaging and other materials.*

- *Develop, manufacture, and market products that are safe for their intended use, efficient in their use of energy, protective of the environment, and that can be reused, recycled or disposed of safely.*
- *Use development and manufacturing processes that do not adversely affect the environment, including developing and improving operations and technologies to minimize waste, prevent air, water, and other pollution, minimize health and safety risks, and dispose of waste safely and responsibly.*
- *Ensure the responsible use of energy throughout our business, including conserving energy, improving energy efficiency, and giving preference to renewable over non-renewable energy sources when feasible.*
- *Participate in efforts to improve environmental protection and understanding around the world and share appropriate pollution prevention technology, knowledge and methods.*
- *Utilize IBM products, services and expertise around the world to assist in the development of solutions to environmental problems.*
- *Meet or exceed all applicable government requirements and voluntary requirements to which IBM subscribes. Set and adhere to stringent requirements of our own no matter where in the world the company does business.*
- *Strive to continually improve IBM's Environmental management system and performance, and periodically issue progress reports to the general public.*
- *Conduct rigorous audits and self-assessments of IBM's compliance with this policy, measure progress of IBM's environmental affairs performance, and report periodically to the Board of Directors.*

Every employee and every contractor on IBM premises is expected to follow this policy and to report any environmental, health, or safety concern to IBM management. Managers are expected to take prompt action."

I believe that this is an extremely solid demonstration of IBM's honest commitment to being a good corporate citizen.

Take this seriously. Spend time with your associates and define the policies that should govern the development of your company. Express them in a language that is adapted to your particular circumstances and communicate them to your employees and others to whom they may concern.

Corporate Culture

All companies and organizations have a culture. Culture for a company is—as it is for a nation—something that is created over its lifespan, a fabric that keeps the organization together, particularly in bad times. It is a result of the history, the founder and the industry and environment it is operating in. Furthermore, it is a result of its customers, its business practices, its owners, its management, its employees, its market etc. If you do not worry about the culture, you get the corporate culture that you get. The other approach is to have a clear opinion of what kind of culture that you want and then you work conscientiously to create the culture that you want to have. The first thing that you could do is to identify the most important factors you want your culture to have. In one company that I worked with we chose the following words to describe our culture:

- Profitability
- Achievement orientation
- Control
- Quality and excellence
- Inclination for and ability to change
- Customer focus
- Respect for the individuals in the organization
- Communication
- High ethical standards
- Recognition of the fact that the employees represent a tremendous potential

In practical life the distinction between corporate values and corporate culture is not clear. When we talk about culture and values we are often talking about the same things. Whether you want to present this as one or two dimensions, I believe that your intellectual exercise to determine what they are should be done in a way that make it logic for your setting and company.

On a closing note, I would like to quote Jens P. Heyerdahl—a very respected and successful Norwegian industrialist. He ran Orkla for 25 years and took it from being a small mining company to become one of the leading Norwegian industrial conglomerates with activities in a number of industries. In an interview he was asked:

"Do you focus on the corporate culture?"

Answered Mr. Heyerdahl: "That (the culture) is the most important value in a corporation. The analysts wave their analyses in order to make the shares of a company look attractive. I look at the management's values and corporate culture. That's where you find the long-term value. First comes human capital, then organizational capital and finally financial capital. Those who focus on this—and in this order—have understood it. To invest in attitudes are the best guarantee for a long life. When we get union representatives to speak as if they were managers of the company, we have made it" . . . . *"It is also important to speak with your employees, have compassion and understand the life of your people. That creates a corporate culture that can sustain black days".* Mind Mr. Heyerdahl's words.

Spend time together with your employees, your management group, your colleagues, the board and also the owners to develop your Mission, Vision, Values, Policies and Culture. Let them also help you identify your Core Competencies. In the long run it will be very helpful for you all in adding value to your company. Apply the techniques that you have learned—like brainstorming and mindmapping—in order to get the best possible result.

IV

Financial Overview and Terminology

What Did Mao Say?

"Have a head for figures." That is to say, we must attend to the quantitative aspects of a situation or problem and make a basic quantitative analysis. Every quality manifests itself in a certain quantity, and without quantity there can be no quality. To this day many of our comrades do not understand that they must attend to the quantitative aspects of things—the basic statistics, the main percentages and the quantitative limits that determine the quality of things. They have no "figures" in their heads and as a result cannot help make mistakes.

"Methods of Work of Party Committees" (March 13, 1949), Selected Works, Vol. IV, pp. 379-80. LRB 111.

Diligence and frugality should be practiced in running factories and shops and all state-owned, co-operative and other enterprises. The principle of diligence and frugality should be observed in everything. This principle of economy is one of the basic principles of socialist economics. China is a big country, but she is still very poor. It will take several decades to make China prosperous. Even then we will still have to observe the principle of diligence and frugality. But it is in the coming few decades, during the present series of five-year-plans, that we must particularly advocate diligence and frugality, that we must pay special attention to economy.

Introductory note to "Running a Co-operative Diligently and Frugally" (1955), The Socialist Upsurge in China's Countryside, Chinese ed.,Vol. I. LRB 187.

Wherever we happen to be, we must treasure our manpower and material resources, and must not take a short view and indulge in wastefulness and extravagance. Wherever we are from the very first year of our work we must bear in mind the many years to come, the protracted war that must be maintained, the counter-offensive, and the work of reconstruction after the enemy's expulsion. On the one hand, never be wasteful and extravagant; on the other actively expand production. Previously, in some places people suffered a great deal because they did not take the long view and neglected economy in manpower and expansion of production. The lesson is there and attention must be called to it.

"We Must Learn to Do Economic Work" (January 10, 1945), Selected Works, Vol. III, p. 244. LRB 185.

In order to speed up this restoration and development (of agricultural production and industrial production in small towns) we must do our utmost, in the course of our struggle for the abolition of the feudal system, to preserve means of production and of livelihood, take resolute measures against anyone's destroying or wasting them, oppose extravagant eating and drinking and pay attention to thrift and economy.

"Speech at a Conference of Cadres in the Shansi-Suiyuan Liberated Area" (April 1, 1948), Selected Works, Vol. IV, p. 138. LRB 188.

Thrift should be the guiding principle in our Government expenditure. It should be made clear to all Government workers that corruption and waste are very great crimes. Our campaign against corruption and waste have already achieved some results, bur further efforts are required. Our system of accounting must be guided by the principle of saving every copper for the war effort, for the revolutionary cause and for our economic reconstruction.

"Our Economic Policy" (January 23, 1934), Selected Works, Vol. I, p. 145. LRB 189.

Profit and Loss Statement

The Profit and Loss Statement—also called the Income Statement—shows the financial records of the company activities over a period—normally one year. In addition to showing how the performance has been, it may also serve as a valuable tool in anticipating how well the company may do in the future. The statement becomes particularly valuable in anticipating future income and expenses if you have a record of several years back in time. The Profit and Loss Statement matches the amounts received from selling the goods, services and other items against all the costs and expenses incurred in order to operate the company. After having recorded the income, one records the cost of goods sold and expenses such as salaries and compensation cost, rent, supplies, depreciation etc.

- **Revenue** is the money that the company receives for the goods and services it has sold to its customers. If there are several revenue types it is possible to determine the relative size of each revenue source and their growth rate from year to year.
- **Costs of Goods Sold** are the elements of cost that are incurred in order to produce the products or services that the company is marketing.
- **Gross Profit** is the difference between the revenue that has been billed to the customers and the costs associated with the production or purchase of them.
- **Operating Expenses** are expenses that cannot be directly related to a specific product or service. They normally comprise two types: **Selling** and **Administration**. Both these categories normally include Salaries and Compensation, overhead including depreciation expenses for the fixed assets that they utilize like buildings, office equipment, transportation equipment, office supplies, distribution costs, advertising and promotion, travel expenses etc.
- **Operating Result (Operating Income)** is the revenue minus cost of goods sold minus operating expenses and expresses the result of the ordinary activities of the company.
- Additional revenue may come from interest earned on cash deposits or dividends from stocks or bonds that are held in other companies and additional expense items incurred as a result of loans, drawing rights

or other obligations. These are gathered in a group called **Net Finance** or **Other Income and Expenses**

- **Net Profit (Earnings, Income) before Tax** is the result that we get after having taken into consideration all the plus factors (the income items) and deducted all costs and expenses (the minus factors).
- **Tax.** Thereafter follow the taxes that are owed on the Income—while Social Security, Real Estate taxes, Sales Taxes etc. are included in the Cost or Expense items.
- **Net After Tax** is the "bottom line" result of the period's activities from a financial point of view. The size of this number is a function of many factors—what type of business one is in, the efficiency with which we are operating, the intensity of the competition in the markets that we are operating in as well as the economic conditions in the area in which we are operating.

Profit and Loss					
			Year 1	**Year 2**	**Year 3**
Total Revenue			1 000	1 100	1 250
Cost of goods sold			500	550	625
Gross profit			500	550	625
Operating cost and expense			360	390	430
of which	Payroll expense		180	190	217
	Depreciation		30	35	40
	Other operating expenses		150	165	173
Operating profit			140	160	195
Net finance			10	11	10
Net before tax			130	149	185
Taxes			60	69	85
Net after tax			70	80	100

All the above numbers are expressed in absolute figures. Absolute figures have their limitations if you want to compare your set of figures to different periods, to the budget, to other companies in the same industry, or companies in other industries, in other countries etc. Later in the book I will show you how percentages, ratios, indices etc. provide significant additional understanding of the figures. I already in this context refer to Chairman Mao when he says " . . . . , *the main percentages and the* quantitative *limits that determine the quality of things"*. These few words express things that are extremely important for businessmen and -women in understanding how their enterprise is doing.

The Balance Sheet

The Balance Sheet may be compared to a photograph taken at a particular point in time showing the financial position of the company. The Balance Sheet consists of two main sections. It shows a record of assets. Assets are the economic resources that are owned and controlled by the company. In addition it contains a record of liabilities, which are obligations owed to others (loans, debts, accounts payable) as well as stockholders equity. The stockholders equity represents the investments that the owners have made in the company. A few pages further down you will see the structure and content of the Balance Sheet. Let's look at the detailed content of these two sections.

- **Assets** consist of the following

    a) **Current Assets** are the first element on the Balance Sheet. Current Assets are assets that represent cash or assets that can be converted into cash within the forthcoming 12 months. These are the most important parts of the current assets:

    i. **Cash and Marketable Securities** including petty cash and bank deposits. It also contains stocks and bonds that are held as short term investments.

    ii. **Accounts Receivable** are the items that are billed to the customers but not yet paid. A portion of the accounts receivable are current and another part is overdue—or items that should have been collected as of the date of the Balance Sheet. Another way of defining the accounts receivable is that they represent the difference between income recorded and the cash that actually has been paid by the customers.

    iii. **Inventories** are the goods that are kept on hand in order to meet the customer demand and to have an uninterrupted flow of operations. They consist of raw materials, semi-raw materials, supplies, work in progress, finished goods and parts for maintenance and repair.

b) **Fixed Assets** consist of those resources that will be used over a multiple of years, f. ex.

    i.   Property like land and land improvements. Land improvements are parking lots, roads etc.

    ii.   Real estate consisting of office buildings, manufacturing buildings, sales and head office buildings etc.

    iii.   Equipment—examples are machinery, ICT equipment, PCs, cars, furniture and fixtures etc.

The sum of current and fixed assets equals total assets.

i.   Liabilities and Stockholders Equity

The other section of the Balance Sheet contains the liabilities. They contain liabilities and stockholders equity and represent the sources of funding for all the resources that are described as assets. Let's look closer at these terms:

a) **Liabilities**

    i.   Current Liabilities are defined as those obligations that are due to be paid within the next twelve months. They include bank loans and other debt payable within the next twelve months; accounts payable to suppliers for goods and services that have not yet been paid and other current liabilities—like compensation, benefits etc.

    ii.   Long Term Debt will normally consist of bank loans, and loans from other financial institutions. This type of debt does not have to be repaid within the next 12 months.

b) **Stockholders Equity** contains the following:

    i.   The money paid to the company for the outstanding shares. This is not the current market price, but the price that prevailed at the time of the share issue. This comprises the initial investment and any additional funds that have been raised later through the sale of shares.

ii.   Retained earnings represents the sum of the profits of the companies minus the dividends paid—i.e. the profits that have been reinvested in the company.

As you can see from the charts, the Liabilities and Stockholders Equity equal the Total Assets.

Balance Sheet

	Year 1	Year 2	Year 3
Assets			
Current assets			
Cash	60	55	60
Accounts receivable	190	190	210
Inventories	250	260	280
Other current assets	35	10	10
Total current assets	**535**	**515**	**560**
Fixed assets			
Machinery and equipment	110	110	115
Real estate and properties	210	230	240
Total fixed assets	**320**	**340**	**355**
Total assets	**855**	**855**	**915**

Balance Sheet

	Year 1	Year 2	Year 3
Liabilities and equity			
Current liabilities			
Accounts payable	70	45	45
Other accounts payable	30	25	20
Other current liabilities	60	60	55
Total current liabilities	**160**	**130**	**120**
Long term debt	**130**	**135**	**145**
Equity			
Shareholders paid in capital	165	165	180
Retained earnings	390	425	470
Total fixed assets	**555**	**590**	**650**
Total assets	**845**	**855**	**915**

These two Statements—The Profit and Loss and the Balance Sheet—to a large extent show what the authorities in most countries require companies to report when they submit their accounting results to a central register. Over and above the numbers, the companies are also required to submit a report where they comment on the various types of issues. The legal requirements are of course different—but in western countries the Income Statement, The Balance Sheet Statement and the Annual Report are what the authorities require.

For internal purposes the reports can look different, i.e. have a content that is different. Firstly, management wants to have more details than are found in these reports. Furthermore, the reason can be that a certain type of business requires the management to focus differently. The legal requirements for depreciation might not suit our type of business. Internal reporting rules might differ and therefore create other requirements. A corporation that operates in many countries will want a standard set of rules to facilitate comparisons from country to country. There might be internal rules for booking revenue that are special as a result of the nature of the business that also might lead to deviations from the statutory requirements.

Cash Flow Statement

One of the main challenges for most companies is the cash flow and we are going to debate this more later in the book when we talk about liquidity. However, as part of the formal reports that are required in most countries we have a statement that shows how funds (Cash) are being generated and how these funds are being used. This statement is called Funds Flow Statement, Sources and Uses of Funds, Statement of Source and Application of Funds etc.

Let's look at such a statement:

Sources and Application of Funds			
	Year 1	Year 2	Year 3
Cash at the beginning of year	60	60	80
Funds from operations			
Sources of funds			
Net earnings after tax	90	100	120
Depreciation	65	70	75
Total	155	170	195
Uses of funds			
Capital investments	(80)	(85)	(110)
Other	(30)	(25)	(30)
Total	(110)	(110)	(140)
Net from operations	45	60	55
External financing			
Loans payable	(5)	(10)	(15)
New long term debt	25	40	25
Total	20	30	10
New share capital	5	10	15
Dividends paid	(40)	(45)	(55)
Taxes to be paid	(30)	(35)	(40)
Cash at the end of year	60	80	65

How to Analyze the Income Statement and Balance Sheet

If you only look at the Income Statement as they have been presented above, you will see that they only contain absolute figures. With only these figures you are missing a lot of important facts that could help you understand the quality of the figures, the development over time, comparisons with other companies in the same industry or companies in other industries etc. To do this it is necessary to develop ratios, percentages and indexes etc. With such figures you will get much more meaningful information about the situation compared to the situation where you only look at the absolute figures.

Look at the Profit and Loss statements a few pages further down. There you will find two versions of the same Profit and Loss statement. The only—but important—differences you see are that to the right there are a number of ratios and percentages that provide more knowledge about the company figures compared to what you get by looking at the absolute figures that you find in the table to the left.

There are a number of ratios that can be applied depending on the purpose of our analysis. Below find show some of those most commonly used related to financials of a corporation.

I am only going to show some of the most common ways to measure financial figures. Many such measurements have limitations. Nevertheless, it is important for a company management to develop a set of ratios that are meaningful for its stakeholders. The following are some of the considerations that should be made when you determine what *your* company's ratios should be:

- Linked to value creation and management decisions
- Simple and pedagogical—in other words they should be easy to understand
- Comprehensive
- Allow for comparisons
- Meaningful for all operational managers, top management, the Board, the shareholders
- Motivational

My experience is that it is more important to find some simple measurements to focus on rather than develop some fancy theoretical measurements that only a few comprehend. In one company we developed a ratio that everybody understood and that everybody was able to determine their contribution to. This had a tremendous impact on the business and the way that we focused because the attainment of the goal for this one ratio made us attain a number of others at the same time.

Let's look at some of the most common ratios. Financial analysts use these ratios when they evaluate the situation of companies that are for sale, listed on the stock exchange or for other purposes. They are pretty universal and general and the basis is the accounting statements that are defined for most businesses. You will therefore learn when we get to the chapter regarding Management Information Systems, that it is also important to develop company specific management information—including ratios—that is tailor-made to a specific company, an industry or other particular situations.

Analyzing the income statements and the balance sheet, we can divide the ratios into profitability ratios, activity ratios and efficiency ratios.

Profitability Ratios		
Cost of goods sold to revenue	$= \dfrac{\text{Cost of goods sold}}{\text{Revenue}}$	These figures (expressed in %) describe the number of cents per sales dollars that is incurred to acquire the goods that are being sold (line 1 and 2) and the number of cents that remain per dollar in sales to cover cost of goods sold, operating expenses and profit (lines 3,4 and 5). The numbers are interesting in themselves, but they are particularly important for two reasons: We can use them to compare the ratios that we had in previous years. They also facilitate a comparison with other companies in the same industry or in different industries. If the **profit ratios** are going up or higher than those of the other companies, that is a healthy sign. If the **expense ratios** are going up or are higher than those of other companies, it is a negative sign.
Expense to revenue	$= \dfrac{\text{Expense}}{\text{Revenue}}$	
Gross profit margin	$= \dfrac{\text{Revenue - Cost of goods sold}}{\text{Revenue}}$	
Operating margin	$= \dfrac{\text{Revenue - (Cost of goods sold - Expenses)}}{\text{Revenue}}$	
NBT margin	$= \dfrac{\text{Net (earnings) before tax}}{\text{Revenue}}$	

Activity Ratios			
Collection period	=	Accounts receivable / (Revenue/360)	This ratio is also called Days of Sales Outstanding or Accounts Payable Collection Period. It measures how many days on the average it takes to collect an average invoice.
Inventory turnover	=	Cost of goods and services / ((Inventory 1/1+Inventory 31/12)/2)	This ratio compares average inventory to cost of goods and services sold. It is an indication of How fast inventory is converted so that it can generate revenue and ensure cash flow
Asset turnover	=	Revenue / ((Total assets 1/1+ Total assets 31/12)/2)	This is a ratio that tells us how many times we turn over our assets in a given year. The faster the better. However, this will vary depending on the industry and type of business we are in.
Net working capital	=	Current assets - Current liabilities	Represents the amount that is free and clear after all current debt is paid off. Determines a company's ability to meet its obligations, expand its volume and take advantage of opportunities.
Current ratio	=	Current assets / Current liabilities	Measures the corporation's ability to pay the short-term liabilities. It should as a minimum be 1, but for stable companies it is expected that this ratio is at least 1,5.
Quick assets	=	Current assets - Inventories	These assets make it possible for you to meet an unexpected emergency because they can be quickly converted into cash.
Quick ratio	=	Quick assets / Current liabilities	This is a rigorous and important test of a company's ability to meet its immediate obligations.
Equity ratio (solidity)	=	Share capital + Retained earnings / (Total equity + Debt)	Shows how much of the total capital that is covered by the equity. A high equity ratio strengthens the corporation's possibility of raising cash through sales of assets or establishing collateral for loans.
Debt ratio	=	Current liabilities + Long term debt / Total equity	Indicates how many $ in debt there are per $ in equity.

Efficiency Ratios			
Return on total assets	=	Net after tax ---------------------------- Average total assets	
Controllable assets	=	Accounts receivable, Inventories, Property, plants and equipment	These are the assets that "create/produce" the revenue streams of the company. A business is required to give credit, keep inventories and have properties, plants and equipment to "produce" the products and services that they provide their customers with.
Return on controllable assets (ROCA)	=	Net after tax ---------------------------------- Average Controllable Assets	This ratio shows the yield on the company's "producing" assets.
EBIDTA— Earnings before depreciation, interest, taxes and amortization	=	Net after tax + Taxes + Interest expenses + Depreciation	This is an approximate measure of a company's operating cash flow based on data from the company's income statement. It is calculated by looking at earnings before the deduction of interest expenses, taxes, depreciation and amortization.
EBIDTA to revenue	=	EBIDTA ------------------X 100 Revenue	EBIDTA in percent of revenue measures the company's earnings strictly on their operations and facilitates comparisons across industries because the depreciation of significant assets and high interest payments due to loans are eliminated.
Return on equity	=	Operating income -- Share capital + Retained earnings	Shows the results of the normal activities of the company after deduction of finance income and expense, extraordinary items and taxes compared to the equity. Should—as a minimum—be the bank interest plus a risk premium of 2-3%.
Cash flow	=	Net before taxes - Taxes + Depreciation -- Revenue	Describes how much each revenue dollar generates in cash. This expresses the company's leverage.

Let us look at the two profit and loss statements that you find a few lines further down. The second table contains a lot more information than what you find in the preceding table. The table has been enriched by percentages and you get much more information than what you get when you look at the table with the absolute figures only. I like to say they express the quality of the numbers. They allow you to compare today's situation with past periods—or future periods if you have done the figures. Let's take an example. If the expense to revenue ratio increases from one year to the next, you have an indication of a deteriorating quality and all things being equal, this deterioration will have a negative impact on your profit margin. And you have the opposite if f.ex. the gross profit margin is going up, then your cost of goods and services sold is a smaller portion of the total revenue than was the case the year before. Consequently, your profit margin goes up.

In the columns next to the absolute figures, you see numbers that indicate the percentage change from year to year. My golden rule is that cost and expense should increase percentagewise less than the increase in revenue.

I cannot stress enough the importance of applying these percentages as a minimum in order to make comparisons and simply to understand your business better than you do without them.

Basic Profit and Loss Data				
			Year 1	Year 2
Total Revenue			9 299	11 220
Cost of goods sold			(4 563)	(5 296)
Gross Profit			4 736	5 924
Operating Cost and Expenses			(2 524)	(3 091)
Of which				
Payroll Expenses			(1 612)	(2 002)
Depreciation			(275)	(300)
Other Operating Expenses			(637)	(789)
Operating Profit			2 212	2 833
Net Finance			(40)	(120)
Net Before Tax			2 172	2 713
Taxes			(270)	(350)
Net After Tax			1 902	2 363

Enriched Profit & Loss Figures	Year 1	Year 2	Year 2/Year 1	
	MUSD	MUSD	MUSD	Index
Total Revenue	9 299	11 220	1 921	120,7 %
Cost of goods sold	(4 563)	(5 296)	(733)	116,1 %
% of revenue	-49,1 %	-47,2 %	1,9 %	
Gross Profit	4 736	5 924	1 188	125,1 %
% of revenue	50,9 %	52,8 %	1,9 %	
Operating Cost and Expenses	(2 524)	(3 091)	-567	122,5 %
% of revenue	-27,1 %	-27,5 %	-0,4 %	
Of which				
Payroll Expenses	(1 612)	(2 002)	(390)	124,2 %
% of revenue	-17,3 %	-17,8 %	-0,5 %	
Depreciation	(275)	(300)	(25)	109,1 %
% of revenue	-3,0 %	-2,7 %	0,3 %	
Other Operating Expenses	(637)	(789)	(152)	123,9 %
% of revenue	-6,9 %	-7,0 %	-0,2 %	
Operating Profit	2 212	2 833	621	128,1 %
% of revenue	23,8 %	25,2 %	1,5 %	
Net Finance	-40	-120	-80	300,0 %
% of revenue	-0,4 %	-1,1 %	-0,6 %	
Net Before Tax	2 172	2 713	541	124,9 %
% of revenue	23,4 %	24,2 %	0,8 %	
Taxes	(270)	(350)	(80)	129,6 %
% of revenue	-2,9 %	-3,1 %	-0,2 %	
Net After Tax	1 902	2 363	461	124,2 %
% of revenue	20,5 %	21,1 %	0,6 %	

The total revenue increase by 20,7 %, while the cost of goods and services sold increase by 16,1 %. The implication of this is that the gross profit margin goes up by 1,9 points.

The operating cost increases by 22,5 % and the ratio to revenue consequently deteriorates by 0,4 %. It is particularly the payroll expenses and other operating expenses that contribute to this.

Despite the deterioration in operating expenses, the revenue growth and the improved cost of goods sold result in a net profit margin that goes up by 0,6 %, while the absolute figure increases as much as 24,9 %.

I cannot but agree with Chairman Mao in the following statement:

"Have a head for figures." That is to say, we must attend to the quantitative aspects of a situation or problem and make a basic quantitative analysis. Every quality manifests itself in a certain quantity, and without quantity there can be no quality. To this day many of our comrades do not understand that they must attend to the quantitative aspects of things—the basic statistics, the main percentages and the quantitative limits that determine the quality of things. They have no "figures" in their heads and as a result cannot help make mistakes.

The ratios described above respond to the requirements that he mentions in the above statement.

V

The Three Stages of Your Company's Route to Success

Whether you start a new company or run a mature company, three terms are extremely important if you want to survive in the long run and be able to concentrate on the future of the company rather than looking back over your shoulder and being preoccupied with matters that hardly bring your company forward towards your vision and goals. There are numerous examples of companies that have not grasped the importance of these terms.

If you emphasize growth without having control or being profitable, you are almost certain to fail. Therefore

1. Control
2. Profitability
3. Growth

are three terms that you should focus on and—mind you—in that order. On the following pages and in most of the rest of the book I would like to explain what I mean by each of these terms.

Let us look at a chart that explains the content of and relationship between these three phases before we continue:

Your Company's Route to Success

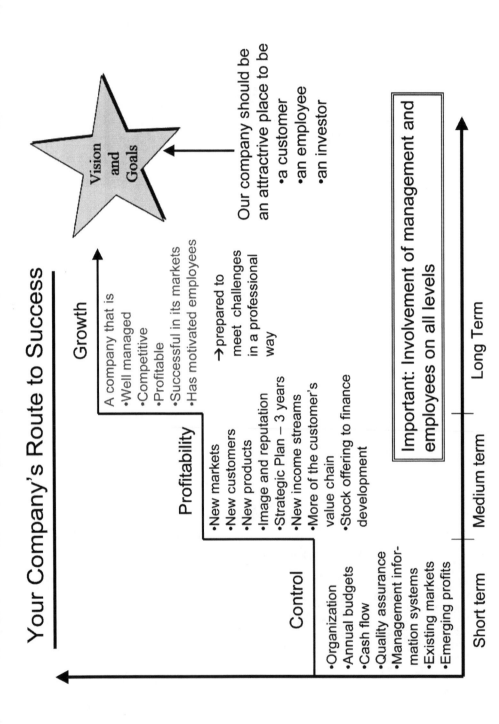

Vision and Goals

Our company should be an attractive place to be
- a customer
- an employee
- an investor

Growth

A company that is
- Well managed
- Competitive
- Profitable
- Successful in its markets
- Has motivated employees

→ prepared to meet challenges in a professional way

Profitability

- New markets
- New customers
- New products
- Image and reputation
- Strategic Plan – 3 years
- New income streams
- More of the customer's value chain
- Stock offering to finance development

Control

- Organization
- Annual budgets
- Cash flow
- Quality assurance
- Management information systems
- Existing markets
- Emerging profits

Short term | Medium term | Long Term

Important: Involvement of management and employees on all levels

1

The Control Phase

In this periode of your company's development it is important to put the basics in place. You need an organization with key people that understand their roles, annual budgets and a strongest possible cash flow control since this is a period in which funds normally are scarce and you are very uncertain of the results. At this stage you should emphasize quality control so that what you produce and deliver to customers or present to potential partners is as good as possible. You need to have some simple Management Information Systems in place to monitor your progress. As far as markets are concerned, you should probably concentrate on existing, local markets that are not too expensive to develop. Through this you should be able to have what we call an emerging profitability.

Organization

What Did Mao Say?

In the sphere of organization, ensure democracy under centralized guidance. It should be done on the following lines:

1. *The leading bodies of the Party must give a correct line of guidance and find solutions when problems arise, in order to establish themselves as centres of leadership.*
2. *The higher bodies must be familiar with the situation in the lower bodies and with the life of the masses so as to have an objective basis for correct guidance.*
3. *No Party organization at any level should make casual decisions in solving problems. Once a decision is reached, it must be firmly carried out.*
4. *All decisions of any importance made by the Party's higher bodies must be promptly transmitted to the lower bodies and the Party rank and file . . . .*
5. *The lower bodies of the Party and the Party rank and file must discuss the higher bodies' directives in detail in order to understand their meaning thoroughly and decide on the methods of carrying them out.*

"On Correcting Mistaken Ideas in the Party" (December 1929)
Selected Works, Vol. I p. 109. LRB 116.

A leading group that is genuinely united and is linked with the masses can gradually be formed only in the process of mass struggle, and not in isolation from it. In the process of a great struggle, the composition of the leading group in most cases should not cannot remain entirely unchanged throughout the initial, the middle and the final stages; the activists who come forward in the course of the struggle must constantly be promoted to replace those original members of the leading group who are inferior by comparison or who have degenerated.

Some Questions Concerning Methods of Leadership (June 1 1943,
Selected Works, Vol. III pp. 206. LRB 118.

There are people in our leading organs in some places who think that it is enough for the leaders alone to know the Party's policy and that there is no need let the masses know them. This is one of the basic reasons why some of our work cannot be done well.

A talk to the Editorial Staff of the Shansi-Suiyuan Daily (April 13, 1948)
Selected Works Vol IV p 241.LRB

"Fewer and better troops and simpler administration". Talks, speeches, articles and resolution should all be concise and to the point. Meetings should also not go on too long.

"Methods of Work of Party Committees" (March 13, 1949),
Selected Works, Vol. IV, p. 377. LRB 113.

Pay attention to uniting and working with comrades who differ with you. This should be borne in mind in the localities and in the army. It also applies to the relations with people outside the Party. We have come together from every corner of the country and should be good at uniting in our work and not only with comrades who hold the same views as we but also with those who hold different views.

"Methods of Work of Party Committees" (March 13, 1949),
Selected Works, Vol. IV, p. 377. LRB 113.

Learn to "play the piano". In playing the piano all ten fingers are in motion; it won't do to move some fingers only and not others. But if all ten fingers press down at once, there is no melody. To produce good music, the ten fingers should move rhythmically and in co-ordination. A Party committee should keep a firm grasp on its central task and at the same time, around the central task, it should unfold the work in other fields. At present, we have to take care of many fields; we must look after the work in all the areas, armed units and departments, and not give our attention to a few problems, to the exclusion of others. Wherever there is a problem, we must put our finger on it, and this is a method we must master. Some play the piano well and some badly, and there is a great difference in the melodies that they produce. Members of the committee must learn to play the piano well.

"Methods of Work of Party Committees" (March 13, 1949),
Selected Works, Vol. IV, p. 377. LRB 110.

We hail from all corners of the country and have joined together for a common revolutionary objective . . . . Our cadres must show concern for every soldier, and all people in the revolutionary ranks must care for each other, must love and help each other.

"Serve the People" (September 8, 1944).
Selected Works Vol III, pp. 227-28. LRB 148.

We must know how to take good care of the cadres. There are several ways of doing so.

First, *give them guidance. This means allowing them a free hand in their works so that they have the courage to assume responsibility and, at the same time giving them timely instructions so that, guided by the party's political line, they are able to make full use of their initiative.*

Second, *raise their level. This means educating them by giving them the opportunity to study so that they can enhance their theoretical understanding and their working ability.*

Third, *check up on their work, and help them sum up their experience, carry forward their achievements and correct their mistakes. To assign work without checking up and to take notice only when serious mistakes are made—that is not the way to take care of cadres.*

Fourth, *in general use the method of persuasion with cadres who have made mistakes, and help them to correct their mistakes. The method of struggle should be confined to those who make serious mistakes and nevertheless refuse to accept the guidance. Here patience is essential. It is wrong lightly to label people "opportunists" or lightly to begin "waging" struggle against them.*

Fifth, *help them with their difficulties. When cadres are in difficulty as a result of illness, straitened means, or domestic or other trouble, we must be sure to give them as much care as possible.*

This is how to take good care of cadres.

"The Role of the Chinese Communist Party in the National War"
(October 1938), Selected Works, Vol II, p. 203. LRB 283.

A communist should never be opinionated or domineering, thinking that he is good in everything while others are good in nothing; he must never shut himself up in his little room, and brag and boast and lord it over others.

"Speech at the Assembly of Representatives of the
Shensi-Kaosu-Ningsia Border Region" (November 21, 1941),
Selected Works, Vol III, p. 33 LRB 274.

> *What we need is an enthusiastic but calm state of mind and intense but orderly work.*
>
> "Problems of Strategy in China's Revolutionary War" (December 1936),
> Selected Works, Vol. I, p. 211 LRB 229.

In an army it is very important to have clear lines of responsibility so that the officers and the soldiers know exactly what their roles and responsibilities are. The reason for this is that the purpose of the army is to conquer, win and annihilate the enemy. Likewise, in a business it is important that the company is organized so that its goals are efficiently pursued and attained with a minimum amount of resources. For this to happen it is important that the employees, irrespective of their place in the organization, know their role, their individual objectives, their group's collective role and objectives and how they impact the objectives of the entire corporation.

It is also very important that the members of the organization regularly meet their managers to agree on objectives and to get feedback on their performance. I am therefore a strong proponent of an organization chart that shows exactly where each individual belongs, who he/she is reporting to, who his/her peers are etc. Obviously, a small company with a few employees probably does not need an organizational structure. But as soon as it grows to more than 5-8 persons I believe that company management should draw an organization chart, put each of the employees in boxes, and give them titles that describe their roles.

An organization chart formalizes the organization to the outside world, it portrays a degree of order and it is probably important for the morale and self-esteem of the employees and the managers. It also signals an efficient use of resources that may be important when you want to convince existing and prospective customers that you are an efficient supplier and when you deal with prospective investors, the banks, your own suppliers, the authorities etc. Furthermore, when you are hiring new employees they would probably appreciate that you can be very clear as to where they will be working.

A few pages below you will find a simple organization chart. This chart shows the relationship between the various layers in the organization of a regular business. Before we look at it let us address two important terms when we talk about organizational structures—Span of control and Number of Layers.

Span of Control is the number of direct reports a manager has reporting to him or her. The number of people can vary considerably—very often as a result of where in the organization we are. At the top of the organization the number of people that report to the general manager could be between 3 and 6—while at the shop floor a supervisor might have 20 people in his/her organization. When you decide on the number of people that should report to a single individual, you have to consider if the number of direct reports make it possible for the manager or supervisor to act as a manager for each person that he/she is responsible for, taking into account regular communication, follow-up, goal setting, performance reviews, and guidance to mention a few of the responsibilities that a person has in the role as manager. **Number of Layers** in the organization is also an important consideration. It is difficult to give clear guidance as far as this is concerned. The tendency, however, is to pursue an organizational structure that has a minimum of layers—i.e. as flat as possible—in order to reduce the number of managers and improve communication in the organization. Ideally—even in large organization—it is considered sufficient to have a maximum of 4-5 layers.

John Hunt in his book *Managing People at Work* states that

o   *There must be clear lines of authority running from the top to the bottom of the organization. The clarity is achieved through the delegation by steps or levels—from the highest executive to the employee whos has least accountability in the organization. It should be possible to trace such a line from the chief executive to every employee. From military language this vertical line is often referred to as the "chain of command".*

o   *No one in the organization should report to more than one supervisor. In other words no one should have more than one superior, boss, manager or whatever the superior is called.*

o   *The accountability and authority of each supervisor and employee should be clearly defined in writing. This enables the individual to know both what is expected of him/her and the limits of the individual's authority as well as it prevents overlapping of tasks and authorities.*

o   *Responsibility should also be coupled with corresponding
    authority.*

o   *The fact that higher authority is responsibile for the acts of
    his subordinates is absolute.*

These rules are based on guidelines established by the Conference Board
in New York. Although they are old, they represent important guidance that
is valuable in our age as well.

Robert Herbold of the Microsoft Corporation warned that too many
layers could dilute creativity when he wrote the following: *"Don't let a
good creative concept or innovation get stifled by passing it through too many
layers of authority in an organization; it is the customers who are the target
audience and real end users of the product, not the management team."* If I
should paraphrase what he is saying, I would say that it is important for
the management not to be to distant from the customers—I cannot agree
with him more.

Here follows a generic organization chart:

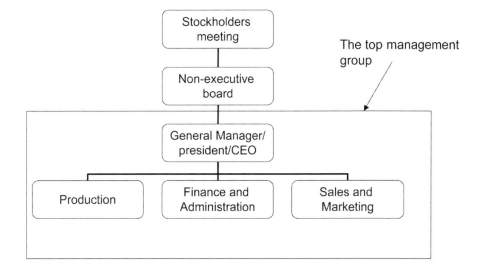

The Stockholders Meeting

- The **stockholders meeting** is the highest body of the organization. After all, the stockholders own the company and "their word is law". The stockholder's meeting is normally held once a year. On the agenda there are important items like

    o The board's (see below) report about the activities of the past year
    o The annual Profit and Loss Statement as well as the Balance Sheet. Normally this is approved by a Certified Public Accountant
    o A proposal for a motion regarding the disposition of the surplus or deficit of the company—including how much that should be paid in dividend to the owners.
    o Election of board members
    o Election of a Certified Public Accountant to audit the books
    o Other important matters that are brought to the meeting's attention
    o Other matters—including changes in the bylaws of the company

From time to time there is a need to hold extraordinary stockholder meetings to decide on important issues. There are normally rules in the bylaws that describe the condition for calling an extraordinary stockholders' meeting. Normally there has to be a certain number of stockholders behind a decision to call a meeting. There are also regulations specifying how far in advance of the meeting that the meeting needs to be called.

The Board

What Did Mao Say?

A school of a hundred people certainly cannot be run well if it does not have a leading group of several people, or a dozen or more, which is formed in accordance with the actual circumstances (and not thrown together artificially) and is composed of the most active, upright and alert of the teachers and the students.

"Some Questions Concerning Methods of Leadership" (June 1 1943), Selected Works, Vol. III pp. 118-19) LRB 166.

Notice of meetings should be given beforehand; this is like issuing a "Notice to Reassure the Public", so that everybody will know what is going to be discussed and what problems are to be solved can make timely preparations. In some places, meetings . . . . are called without first preparing reports and draft resolution, and only when people have arrived for the meeting are makeshifts improvised; this is just like the saying, "Troops and horses have arrived, but food and fodder are not ready", and that is no good. Don't call a meeting in a hurry if the preparations are not completed.

"Methods of Work of Party Committees (March 13, 1949) Selected Works, Vol.IV, p.380 LRB 112.

Place the problems on the table. This should be done not only by the "squad leader", but by the committee members too. Do not talk behind people's backs. Whenever problems arise, place the problem on the table for discussion, take some decisions and the problems will be solved. If problems exist and are not put on the table, they will remain unsolved for a long time and even drag on for years. The "squad leader" and the committee members should show understanding in their relations with each other. Nothing is more important than mutual understanding, support and its regional bureaus and the regional bureau and the area Party Committee.

"Methods of Work of Party Committees" (March 13, 1949) Selected Works, Vol. IV, p.377-78. LRB 108.

> *"Grasp firmly".* This is to say, the Party committee must not merely *"grasp"*, but *"grasp firmly"*, its main task. One can get a grip on something only when it is grasped firmly, without the slightest slackening. Not to grasp firmly is not to grasp at all. Naturally, one cannot get a grip on something with an open hand. When the hand is clenched tightly, there is still no grip. Some of our comrades do grip the main tasks, but their grasp is not firm and so they cannot make a success of their work. It will not do to have no grasp at all, nor will it do if the grasp is not firm.
>
> "Methods of Work of Party Committees" (March 13, 1949)
> Selected Works, Vol. IV, p.377-78. LRB 111.
>
> *"Exchange information".* This means that members of a Party committee should keep each other informed and exchange views on matters that have come to their attention. This is of great importance in achieving a common language. Some fail to do so, and like the people described by Lao Tzu, "do not visit each other all their lives, though the crowing of their cocks and the barking of their dogs are within hearing of each other". The result is that they lack a common language.
>
> "Methods of Work of Party Committees" (March 13, 1949)
> Selected Works, Vol. IV, p.378. LRB 108.

A discussion of a corporation's organization—must include Corporate Governance i.e. the system by which companies are directed or controlled. This has become a matter of interest throughout the world because the corporate boards and directors are accountable for corporate performance and the legal and ethical behavior of the companies that they are managing. All over the world there is an increased emphasis on the responsibility of the organizations that society sees as exercising power.

It is very important to compose the board of a company in such a way that it becomes effective in monitoring the operations of the company. When you select the Board of directors you should take into consideration the personal qualities, the educational background and business experience of each individual. Personal independence and integrity are also very important qualities. The objective is to compose a competent group with a diverse background so that the Board of directors becomes effective in managing and monitoring the performance and development of the company. Only under very special circumstances should the Chief Executive and the Chairman be the same person. As Percy Barnevik—the former head of ABB—puts it: *"Even if you are seen as a strong, maybe a dictatorial chief executive it makes you stronger, not weaker to have a non-executive chairman."*

Very often these important points are not taken into consideration when corporations pick members for their non-executive boards. Personal relationships, kinship, ongoing business relationships etc. should immediately exclude a person from being eligible for a position on the board. There are many reasons for this, but the most important is that such relationships make it difficult to exercise independent judgement in carrying out responsibilities. Just think about a situation where the board discusses the performance of the General Manager. If you don't have an arm's lengths distance to the individual, how can you participate independently in such a discussion?

In the past it used to be the old boys' network that determined who should be on the board. Today the selection criteria—particularly in light of the corporate governance discussion—takes into consideration that the board members are expected to play a scrutinizing role with the ability to voice their opinions in a critical, but constructive tone.

An important role for the board is that they supervise the General Manager of the company. This is a factor that needs to be taken into consideration.

Looking at the composition of the board, you very often find executives that serve on a number of other boards in addition to holding a busy executive position. The justification of this is that they have a network and can be important door openers for the company. This might be right, but I think you should be mindful of the fact that the day only has 24 hours for everybody and that those with a well-known name do very often not have the time necessary to add value to a board. A board membership is not only participation in meetings; it also requires time for preparation. I therefore believe that when you recruit for the board you should not only look for the people that are at the top—but those that are just under the surface, hungry to advance. Here you should follow Chairman Mao's guidance about firmly grasping what the business is all about. My experience is that often the board members are not sufficiently conversant with important terminology, the organization, the products and services etc. and consequently steal time from more important matters because they have to have routine and basic matters explained to them in meeting after meeting.

Before the process of selecting a new board member starts, the board or the owners should jointly clearly specify the requirements of the ideal person. This process could start with the identification of the gaps in experience and

knowledge that exist in today's board. It takes time to build an effective board
for the chairman as well as for the board and it does not necessarily mean
that having competent persons sitting around the board table constitute an
effective and value-adding board. In a well-functioning board there is "good
chemistry" between the board members—they have respect for each other
despite diverse backgrounds and differences of opinion. The existence of a
good sense of humor and the ability to crack a joke are "lubricating agents"
for the process—particularly when the "going gets tough".

The chairman plays an important role. The way he conducts the meeting
and plays his role can be very decisive for the board's effectiveness. The
chairman can create an open tone around the table where there is a value-
adding debate or he can stifle the discussion.

Percy Barnevik—the head of ABB—said: *"The board must be able to
access all the relevant information, discuss matters openly, form an opinion and
act to influence management. That is what it's there for."* That is another way
of expressing the importance of being independent.

As A. Daniel Mailand—the head of Egon Zehnder International put it:
*". . . compiling a board with the ideal blend of knowledge and skills can provide the
expertise they need to chart the right strategic course in an increasingly global market".*
In this context it is very important to point out that in many countries there is a
drive to increase the number of women on the boards as well as minority group
representation. Other places it is normal for the employees to have representatives
on the board. This is particularly the case in Scandinavia, Germany and the
Netherlands. In the two latter countries it is also legally defined that corporations
have a social function in addition to their role as a business organization.

One thing I would warn against is the selection of board members in
order to get free consulting assistance.

In large corporations, small committees—consisting of 3-5 members—are
formed in addition to the board. Very often these committees consist of outside
non-executive board members. Examples of such committees are:

o   Audit Committee
o   Compensation Committee
o   Strategy Committee
o   Technology Committee
o   ICT Committee
o   Executive Selection Committee

In order for the meetings to be effective the members should in advance receive papers and reports that make it possible for them to prepare themselves for the meeting. Such papers could be reports, business cases, proposals, minutes etc. Under normal circumstances these documents should be in the hands of the board members one week in advance of the meeting.

As to the venue of board meetings, they should not only take place at headquarters—but from time to time out in the field where the board members can see for themselves what the local situation is in a division or in a regional office. This is also an opportunity to meet the local management and assess its quality. At the same time it is motivating for the local management to get this type of attention.

As to the frequency of the board meetings it could under normal circumstances, be anything between 4-12 times a year. Under unusual circumstances—when the company is under the guns for positive or negative reasons—it might be appropriate to have board meetings every day or every week. The latter should only occur for a limited period of time because it is very important that the board does not take over the operational responsibilities of the company. That is the responsibility of the management. Board meetings do not necessarily have to be conducted face-to-face. Telephone meetings are often a very effective time– and cost-saving way of getting together. The meetings should typically have an agenda that consist of regular items like:

1. Notice about the meeting
2. Agenda
3. Minutes from the previous meeting
4. Business results year-to-date (volumes and financials)
5. Forecasts—results and cash flow
6. Important strategic issues like future plans and investments
7. Any other business

The meetings should be minutted with a concentration of the resolutions that have been passed. The minutes should be signed by all the board members and kept in a paginated protocol and kept under lock. It is a very important document, particularly if the company runs into difficulties and must face legal proceedings.

Top Management

What did Mao Say?

A commander's correct dispositions stem from his correct decisions, his correct decisions from his correct judgements, and his correct judgements stem from a thorough and necessary reconnaissance and from pondering on and piecing together the data of various kinds gathered through reconnaissance. He applies all possible and necessary methods of reconnaissance, and ponders on the information gathered about the enemy's situation. Discarding the dross and selecting the essential, eliminating the false and retaining the true, proceeding from the one to the other and from the outside to the inside; then, he takes conditions on his own side into account and makes a study of both sides and their interrelations, thereby forming his judgements, making up his mind and working out his plans. Such is the complete process of knowing a situation which a military man goes through before he formulates a strategic plan, a campaign plan or a battle plan.

"Problems of Strategy in China's Revolutionary War" (December 1936),
Selected Works, Vol. I, p. 188. LRB 235.

For a military school, the most important question is the selection of a director and instructors and the adoption of an educational policy.

"Problems of Strategy in China's Revolutionary War" (December 1936)
Selected Works, Vol. I, p. 185 LRB 166.

A school of a hundred people certainly cannot be run well if it does not have a leading group of several people, or a dozen or more, which is formed in accordance with the actual circumstances (and not thrown together artificially) and is composed of the most active, upright and alert of the teachers and the students.

"Some Questions Concerning Methods of Leadership" (June, 1 1943),
Selected Works, Vol. III, pp. 118-19. LRB 166.

"Exchange information". This means that members of a Party committee should keep each other informed and exchange views on matters that have come to their attention. This is of great importance in achieving a common language. Some fail to do so, and like the people described by Lao Tzu, "do not visit each other all their lives, though the crowing of their cocks and the barking of their dogs are within hearing of each other". The result is that they lack a common language.

"Methods of Work of Party Committees" (March 13, 1949), Selected Works, Vol. IV, p.378. LRB 108.

A leading group that is genuinely united and is linked with the masses can gradually be formed only in the process of mass struggle, and not in isolation from it. In the process of a great struggle, the composition of the leading group in most cases should not and cannot remain entirely unchanged throughout the initial, the middle and the final stages; the activists who come forward in the course of the struggle must constantly be promoted to replace those original members of the leading group who are inferior by comparison or who have degenerated.

"Some Questions Concerning Methods of Leadership" (June 1, 1943), Selected Works, Vol. III. p. 118. LRB 285

One of the most important tasks of the board is to attract, develop and retain competent management talent, especially the President, the General Manager, the Managing Director or whatever the title of the Chief Executive Officer is. There is absolutely no doubt that the top man is decisive for the development of the company. If you don't have a person at the helm that has the right skills—theoretical background, practical experience, personal qualities—you are off to a bad start.

Professor **Klaus Schwab** says in an interview in EZI Focus Corporate Governance Fall 97:

"The management factor is decisive. Global competitiveness is invariably influenced by management capabilities within a specific branch (industry) or corporation. This is because the ability to identify negative factors at an early stage and transform them rapidly into positive parameters is one of the crucial strengths in international

competition. Moreover, the management factor alone will determine
whether the required market leadership is achieved or not.

. . . . above and beyond core competencies, management must be
able to define where a corporation's market opportunities lie. We are
dealing here with a dynamic process that calls for dynamic, integrated
thinking because the background conditions are forever changing. So,
management needs to display exceptional flexibility in an approach
that combines mental flexibility, with a personal command of electronic
management information systems.

. . . . Long-term management orientation must be coordinated
with an ongoing improvement in efficiency and flexible deployment
mechanisms. In general the pressure on top management to achieve
short-term results is increasing, which is sure to lead to shorter
assignments at the top level."

Or as **Percy Barnevik**—the head of ABB—expressed it:

". . . . whatever they (top managers) bring with them in their theoretical
backpack is going to be useful . . . . but when you look at the companies
that succeed they don't have some fantastic strategy that nobody else had.
What they have is a way of mobilizing people, getting them to pull in
the same direction, breathing a stretch mentality in the same direction, a
corporate culture geared to change. The key to success is 90% execution,
10% strategy. And in these 10% there is maybe 2% that is analysis, data,
models and tools, while the remaining eight is guts and gut feeling".

Nepotism—giving preferential treatment to people that are close to the
decision maker—as the basis for appointment of the top men or women in
an organization is very damaging and completely unacceptable. The only
basis for employment, promotion, changes in compensation and benefits are
competence and professionalism.

When the board is faced with the situation of hiring new management,
they have to go through a meticulous process that ascertains that they are
getting the right person(s). If this is a matter about finding the top executive,
I strongly believe that you should use an executive search company. They
have systematic processes, they have a broad network—nationally as well as

internationally—they work in strict confidence, your name does not need to be revealed too early in the process. Their process will typically run along the following path:

- Determine what the needs are

    o What are his/her tasks?
    o What is the situation of the company?
    o What kind of goals do the board and owners have for the future?
    o Are there any particular hardships or unusual conditions that he/she will have to comply with?
    o What is the salary range that you are prepared to accept?

- What kind of person are you therefore looking for?

    o Education
    o Work experience
    o Gender
    o Language capabilities
    o Age
    o Personality traits

- You should also offer a small consideration as to what kind of person are you **not** looking for

- Start the process

    o Ad in the newspaper
    o The search company starts the process

It is extremely important that you make a correct choice. You therefore have to go through a comprehensive process. This is important whenever you make a personnel decision, but extremely important when we talk about the head(s) of the company. This is the person whose skills, competence, personality, energy, creativity, innovative abilities, network, judgements, ability to handle people, ability to handle customers etc. will be decisive for the future. Of course, all the employees are important pawns in the total machinery, but the most important person—as Mao repeatedly emphasizes—is the head. He is holding the banner; behind him the troops stand motivated and united.

It is difficult to describe an exact list of the personality traits that are required for executives nowadays. But let's try to make a list of things that are very important:

Operational Skills

When you search for a new executive, it is extremely important that the individual has a record of operational and managerial experience—not necessarily from the industry that you are in, but at least from an environment that is similar as far as pressures are concerned. He or she should be able to tackle the uncertainties that most companies are facing today and in light of this be able to forecast, recruit, budget, make decisions, forge partnerships and alliances. He/she also needs to develop and maintain the company's entrepreneurial spirit together with a strong focus on operational expertise and control.

Communication Skills

Communication skills are also extremely important for today's executives. There are vast groups of people that the company are dependent upon to be successful. These are employees, customers, investors, the authorities, the press etc. It is important that all these people have the proper perception of your company and can view it positively from the angle that is important for them. These skills are—as you understand from the list in the former sentence—internally as well as externally directed. The broad signal that he is going to convey is a credible message about the company's products and services, the strategic direction, the mission and vision, the policies etc.

Decisionmaking Skills

The extreme pace with which events evolve in today's volatile environment also requires rapid decision-making—often with less information than what more time and analysis could have provided. An executive has to make a decision based on intuition and accept that it is better to make a quick decision that can be improved rather than wait for the perfect decision while your competitors are increasing the distance between you. Investors as well as customers and employees appreciate that new things are happening. An executive's focus and behavior should ascertain that positive vibrations among stakeholders are benefitting his company as well.

Human Relations Skills

Your staff and their competence and skills will increasingly be your most important resource. It is also extremely important for an executive to understand their situation, their dreams and aspirations, their social situation, their personal situation, the out-of-job pressures that they are exposed to, what they are interested in etc. I am not saying that he or she should know this for each individual—that would be impossible. But he should know the situation of the employees as a group as far as these things are concerned. Another word for the same thing is empathy. Empathy stands for understanding, sympathy and compassion. Personally, I believe that to show empathy is one of the most important traits for an executive in his pursuit of motivated and satisfied employees. *In Search of Excellence* by Tom Peters and Robert H. Waterman jr. introduced the expression: *"Management by Walking Around"*. This expression was invented after having studied the traits that were most predominant in some of the world's most successful corporations. As the words signal, the ability to be close to your employees, to talk to them frequently, to understand their situation, to take them seriously, and to listen to them were crucial for the success of these companies. Here we are talking about companies like Hewlett Packard, IBM, Procter and Gamble, Delta Airlines, McDonald's, Johnson and Johnson etc. Having said this, it is also important to note that the top person is the top person. He has to make tough decisions from time to time. Often these are decisions impacting people. Hence, he or she must try to avoid being so close to individuals that he loses independence in a tough situation.

Nobody entirely fits the bill that has been drawn up. When you make the decision to employ someone, you will always have a trade-off between the existence and absence of skills that you would like the candidates to have in the ideal world.

The Main Generic Functions

The Managing Director (President, General Manager) together with the functional managers, constitute the top management of the company. What kind of functions that you need to have in the management group are very much dependent on the type of company that you are running. Therefore it will be very difficult to describe all the alternatives. However, if we were going to look at it generically I would say that there are three important areas that must be represented. They are **Production**, **Sales and Marketing** and **Finance and Administration** and all that these areas entail. Why is that?

Before we answer this rhetoric question let us again look at the generic organization chart, which was shown earlier:

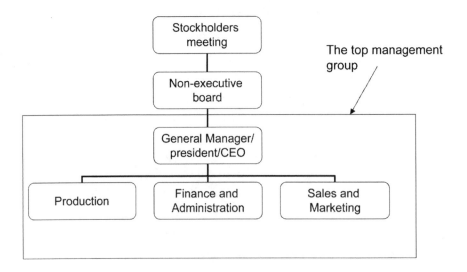

Generic Organization Chart

Production

All companies have to produce something that their customers demand. Through this demand there is a creation of revenue-streams that are the basis for the profitability of the company. Production must in this respect be considered in its widest context. It is very evident for most of us that production is to make objects that are concrete, like a car, an airplane, a bottle, a table, a chair etc. However, to render a bank service, to provide air travel and to perform an operation at a hospital etc. also is a question of production.

Sales and Marketing

We can be world champions in developing and manufacturing products and providing services, but it does not help us a bit if we do not have sales or distribution channels to sell them and an organization to bring them to the customers. These include promotion; advertising in newspapers, on TV and on the internet; they require a sales force, dealer networks, marketing, market analysts etc. In this function a lot of expenses are incurred—but without them it would be impossible to inform the customer of our products' existence, and with no knowledge of our products there would be no sales.

Finance and Administration

Statutory requirements demand that we account for the revenue that we are generating as well as the cost and expense that we are incurring when producing and selling our products and/or services. Consequently, a Finance and Administration function is also an important element in a generic organization. But such a function is also responsible for other tasks like personnel administration, purchasing—except for the raw materials and other components that are part of our products—Information Technology, buildings administration etc.

Keep in mind that above I have been addressing the generic and basic functions of a company. In real life things are more complicated and diversified. In your company it might therefore be logical to have more functions reporting to the head of the company or you would organize things differently based on other considerations. The larger the company becomes, the more specialized the functions will be and the more the departments each of the functions will have. This will be obvious when we further down describe each of the functions in the generic organization.

As stressed above, the general manager and his functional heads constitute the top management of the company. Together they are a closed group that may disagree on important matters—in fact they should disagree in order to get the right dynamic in the group. However, vis á vis the rest of the organization they should appear relatively well concerted and be perceived among the rest of the organization as a group that consists of different characters, but are united as a group. It is important within the company that this group is perceived as working well together and liking each other—despite disagreements of an objective nature. They should speak well of each other and avoid criticizing each other in public. This group, like all managers in a company, is perceived as role models. The rest of the organization will look to them for guidance as to appropriate behavior. If they bend the rules in certain matters, how can they demand that the rest of the company follow the rules, policies and other requirements? It is extremely important for the top management group to be aware of this and act accordingly. Chairman Mao has a number of statements as to the composition of the management group, its behavior and its important function as role models for the rest of the organization.

Production

> **What Did Mao Say?**
>
> *Production by the masses, the interest of the masses, the experience and feelings of the masses—to these the leading cadres should pay constant attention.*
>
> Inscription for a production exhibition sponsored organizations directly under the Central Committee of the Party and the General Headquarters of the Eigth Route Army, Liberation Daily of Yenan, November 24, 1943. LRB 132
>
> *Wherever we happen to be, we must treasure our manpower and material resources, and must not take a short view and indulge in wastefulness and extravagance. Wherever we are, from the very first year of our work we must bear in mind the many years to come, the protracted war that must be maintained, the counter-offensive, and the work of reconstruction after the enemy's expulsion. On the one hand, never be wasteful and extravagant; on the other, actively expand production. Previously, in some places people suffered a great deal because they did not take the long view and neglected economy in manpower and material resources and the expansion of production. The lesson is there and attention must be called to it.*
>
> "We Must Learn to Do Economic Work" (January 10, 1943), Selected Works, Vol. III, p. 144. LRB 187.
>
> *Production by the army for its own support has not only improved the army's living conditions and lightened the burden on people, thereby making it possible to further to expand the army. In addition it has had many side-effects. They are as follows:*
>
> 1. *Improved relations between officers and men. Officers and men work together in production and become brothers*
> 2. *Better attitude to labour . . . . since the army began to produce for its own support, the attitude to labour has improved and loafer ways have been overcome.*
> 3. *Strengthened discipline. Far from weakening discipline in army battle and in army life, labour discipline in production actually strengthens it.*

4. *Improved relations between the army and the people. Once an armed force begins to "keep house" for itself, encroachments upon the property of the people seldom or never occur. As the army and the people exchange labour and help each other in production, the friendship between them is strengthened.*

5. *Less grumbling in the army about the Government and improved relations between the two.*

6. *An impetus to the great production campaign of the people. Once the army engages in production, the need for government and other organizations to do likewise becomes more obvious, and they do so more energetically; also, the need for a universal campaign of the whole people to increase production naturally becomes more obvious and this too is carried on more energetically.*

"On Production by the Army for Its Own Support and the Importance of the Great Movements for Rectification and for Production" (April 27, 1945), Selected Works, Vol. III, pp. 327-28. LRB 190.

In transforming a backward agricultural China into an advanced industrialized country, we are confronted with arduous tasks and our experience is far from adequate. So we must be good at learning.

"Opening Adress at the Eighth National Congress of the Communist Party of China" (September 15, 1956). LRB 304.

Some people say that if the army units go in for production, they will be unable to train or fight and that if the government and other organizations do so, they will be unable to do their own work. This is a false argument. In recent years our army units in the Border Region have undertaken the production on a big scale to provide themselves with ample food and clothing and have simultaneously done their training and conducted their political study and literacy and other courses much more successfully than before, and there is greater unity than ever within the army and the people. While there was a large-scale production campaign at the front last year, great successes were gained in the fighting and in addition an extensive training campaign was started. And thanks to production the personell of the government and other organizations live a better life and work with greater devotion and efficiency; this is the case both in the Border Region and at the front.

"We Must Learn to Do Economic Work" (January 10, 1945), Selected Works, Vol. III, pp. 243-44. LRB 192.

Reading is learning, but applying is also learning and the more important kind of learning at that. Our chief method is to learn warfare through warfare. A person who has had no opportunity to go to school can also learn warfare—he can learn through fighting in war. A revolutionary war is a mass undertaking; it is often not a matter of first learning and then doing, but of doing and then learning, for doing it is itself learning.

"Problems of Strategy in China's Revolutionary War" (December 1936), Selected Works, Vol. I, pp. 189-90. LRB 308.

Those experienced in work must take up study of theory and must read seriously; only then will they be able to systematize and synthesize their experience and raise it to the level of theory, only then will they not mistake their partial experience for universal truth and not commit empiricist errors.

"Rectify the Party's Style of Work", (February 1, 1942) Selected Works, Vol. III. p. 42. LRB 308

Thrift should be the guiding principle in our government expenditure. It should be made clear to all government workers that cooruption and waste are very great crimes. Our campaign against corruption and waste have already achieved some results, but further efforts are required. Our system of accounting must be guided by the principle of saving every copper for the war effort, for the revolutionary cause and for our economic construction.

"Our Economic Policy" (January 23, 1934), Selected Works, Vol. I, p. 145. LRB 189.

Diligence and frugality should be practised running factories and shops and all state-owned, co-operative and other enterprises. The principle of diligence and frugality should be observed in everything. This principle of economy is one of the basic principles of socialist economics. China is a big country, but it is still very poor. It will take several decades to make China prosperous. Even then we will still have to observe the principle of diligence and frugality. But it is in the coming few decades, during the present series of five-year plans, that we must particularly advocate diligence and frugality, that we must pay special attention to economy.

Introductory note to "Running a Co-operative Diligently and Frugally" (1955), The Socialist Upsurge in China's Countryside, Chinese ed., Vol. I. LRB 187.

> *The world is progressing, the future is bright and no one can change this general*
> *trend of history. We should carry on constant propaganda among the people on*
> *the facts of world progress and the bright future ahead so that they will build*
> *their confidence in victory.*
>
> "On the Chungking Negotiations" (October 17, 1945),
> Selected Works, Vol. IV, p. 19. LRB 70.

All companies have to produce something that their customers demand. Through this demand there is a creation of revenue-streams that are the basis for the profitability of the company. Production must in this respect be considered in its widest context. It is very logical if it is a question of manufacturing gadgets or widgets that are concrete things that you can put your hands on like a car, an airplane, a bottle, a table, a chair etc. However, if it's a question about a bank service, air travel, an operation at a hospital etc. it's also a question of production. In some companies these functions would be called operations. To phrase it differently, what I mean by production is the delivery of the product or the service that we are providing and that the customer is willing to pay for. Very often it would be appropriate to include the physical handling and distribution of the products in this part of the organization.

A Norwegian company called Protec Consult works to realize World Class Production in manufacturing environments, where a physical gadget is made and delivered to their clients' customers. In other words, their focus is on the manufacturing and delivery of a physical product to their customers. However, as we go along with their concept as the basis, you will see that the principles that they emphasize—aimed at manufacturing companies—to a large extent apply to the production of services as well.

Protec recommends the following focus on the road to World Class Manufacturing:

o   *Small production series*
o   *Minimal inventories*
o   *Continuous flow of work in progress*
o   *Eradication of errors, rework and customer complaints*
o   *Elimination of all activities that do not contribute to added value*

o *Continuous organizational development and build-up of competence to attain competent and motivated employees*
o *Let employees get ownership to their processes*
o *Identify potential for continuous improvements*
o *Product improvements*

The basic elements in their philosophy is to create an overall understanding for the need for change in the entire organization and realize that it takes time to instill the minds of the employees to accept this. Therefore they start with simple things like the need for orderliness and to be organized in order to work more efficiently. The efficiency work continues with definition of goals. Thereafter they suggest that you evaluate activities in small groups, reduction in "Work in process", introduction of new technology for rapid change. They suggest a Kaizen system for continuous improvements. They suggest so-called Kanban systems to monitor the supply of materials to the production so that (1) the necessary materials are present (2) in the necessary volumes (3) at the right time. In order to reduce down-time of the production equipments and idle employees, preventive maintenance and repair has to be scheduled properly. Discipline at the work-site and quality assurance are very important. Many companies have gained a lot from making the operators responsible for their machinery and work environment in order to achieve maximum efficiency and guarantee production quality and reduce the likelihood for errors in the machinery and the products.

Most companies will gain a lot by developing their suppliers so that they become strategic partners that deliver the right materials at the right time at reasonable prices. With a closely-knit relationship with the suppliers they can be very valuable when you have a problem, when you need to source new materials, or when you need to be more cost-efficient than in the past. In most companies the sales departments and salesmen are given a lot of focus and attention, while there is lesser focus and attention on the purchasing function and the buyers. Given the potential for savings through professional purchasing I believe that many companies should shift their focus and celebrate the purchasing department more than they currently do.

In production there has to be a focus on waste or in other words how you can avoid waste. Protec defines waste as: (1) products with errors, (2) unnecessary processes, (3) waiting, (4) overproduction, (5) inventories that are larger than required, (6) unnecessary transportation and (7) erroneous processes.

Furthermore, in order to attain World Class Manufacturing Protec recommends delegation of authority, efficient production planning and active use of IT-systems and leadership in technology as important measures.

The generic production organization looks like this and the mission of these functions is described below each of them.

The Production Division

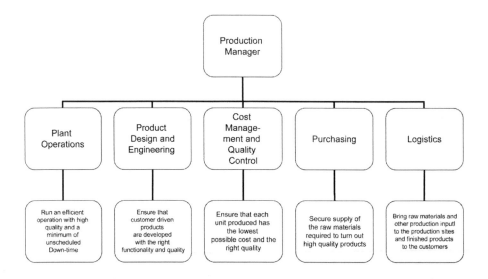

The chart above describes the situation in a manufacturing environment. However, I would like to stress again that the same philosophy reflected in the chart also can be applied to companies delivering (producing) services. Such services could be bank-services, financial services, cleaning, building services, all types of maintenance, transportation, travel agencies, consulting, health care, public services, call centers etc. My point is that when you render services, they have to be delivered flawlessly; the services have to contain what the customers need and expect. They have to be produced at a low cost and be conceived of as high quality. These factors have to be measured regularly through a set of relevant Key Performance Indicators so that unsatisfactory situations can be rectified. A service rendering-organization needs to be staffed with the right number of skilled people, and have adequate equipment like telephone systems, PC-systems etc. In other words, to render services resembles the manufacturing of physical products.

CHAIRMAN MAO'S BUSINESS SCHOOL

Sales and Marketing

What Did Mao Say?

In all mass movements we must make a basic investigation and analysis of the numbers of active supporters, opponents and neutrals and must not decide problems subjectively and without basis.

"Methods of Work of Party Committees" (March 13, 1949)
Selected Works, Vol IV p. 380. LRB 130.

We should go to the masses and learn from them, synthesize their experience into better, articulated principles and methods, then do propaganda among the masses and call upon them to put these principles and methods into practice so as to solve their problems and help them achieve liberation and happiness.

"Get Organized!" (November 29, 1943),
Selected Works, Vol. III, p. 158. LRB 129.

In all the practical work of our party, all correct leadership is necessarily "from the masses, to the masses". This means: take the ideas of the masses (scattered and unsystematic ideas) and concentrate them (through study turn them into systematic and systematic ideas), then go to the masses and propagate and explain these ideas until the masses embrace them as their own, hold fast to them and translate them into action, and test the correctness of these ideas into such action. Then once again concentrate ideas from the masses and once again go to the masses so that the ideas are persevered in and carried through. And so on, over and over again in an endless spiral, with the ideas becoming more correct, more vital and richer each time. Such is the Marxist theory of knowledge.

"Some Questions Concerning Methods of Leadership" (June 2, 1943),
Selected Works, Vol. III, p. 119. LRB 128.

To link oneself with the masses one must act in accordance with the needs and wishes of the masses. All work done for the masses must start from their needs and not from the desire of any individual, however well-intentioned. It often happens that objectively the masses need a certain change, but subjectively, they are not yet conscious of the need, not yet willing or determined to make the change. In such cases we should wait patiently. We should not make the change until, through our work, most of the masses become conscious of the need and are willing and determined to carry it out. Otherwise we shall isolate ourselves from the masses. Unless they are conscious and willing, any kind of work that requires their participation will turn out to be mere formality and will fail. . . . There are two principles here: One is the actual needs of the masses rather than what we fancy they need, and the other is the wishes of the masses, who must make up their own minds instead of our making their minds for them.

"The United Front in Cultural Work" (October 30, 1944),
Selected Works, Vol. III, pp. 236-37. LRB 124.

As for the training courses, the main objective should still be to raise the level of technique in marksmanship, bayoneting, grenade-throwing and the like and the secondary objective should be to raise the level of tactics, while special emphasis should be laid on night operations.

"Policy for Work in the Liberated Areas for 1946" (December 15, 1945),
Selected Works, Vol. IV, p. 76. LRB 169.

Our slogan in training troops is, "Officers teach soldiers, soldiers teach officers and soldiers teach each other". The fighters have a lot of combat experience. The officers should learn from the fighters, and when they have made other people's experience their own, they will be more capable.

"A Talk to the Editorial Staff of the Shansin-Suiyuan Daily" (April 2,
1948), Selected Works, Vol. IV, p. 243. LRB 168.

Production by the masses, the interest of the masses, the experience and feelings of the masses—to these the leading cadres should pay constant attention.

Inscription for a production exhibition sponsored by organizations
directly under the Central Committee of the Party and the
General Headquarters of the Eighth Route Army,
Liberation Daily of Yenan, November 24, 1943. LRB 132.

Let us use the following organization chart as the basis for this discussion:

The Sales and Marketing Division

The simple purpose of sales and marketing is to **attract**, **develop** and **retain** profitable customers for companies. This is a simple definition with a lot of content and implications. We are living in a world where competition is becoming keener and keener and where you have to direct a lot of your resources towards the market in order to generate the revenue that is required.

This means that you have to be obsessed with customer orientation; you have to think customers all the time; you have to be certain that the products that you are delivering are what the customers want; you have to make certain that the quality of your customer service is so good that your customers come back again and again.

This applies whether you are a large or a small company, whether you have big customers or small customers; whether you are selling products or services or both; whether your products are expensive or low-priced.

You have to dialogue with your customers all the time so that they get **your** message and you get **their** message. I am certain that you now are exhausted so let us start to explore this important area. But first let's hear some words from Sir Colin Marshall, former chairman of British Airways: *"In modern business, the vital role of management is to come out of the office and* *the boardroom to the point of sales and service. If those of us who run companies have not got our customers in sight and within earshot all the time, we shall be passed over."* He is so right in the assertion that sales and customer contacts are the responsibilities of top management in a company.

Let us start to discuss what **attract**, **develop** and **retain** profitable customers means in marketing terms.

Attract profitable customers

A popular phrase says that it is seven times more expensive to get a new customer than it is to retain or make a resale to an existing customer. Based on this you could sit back and only harvest from your existing customer base. However, it is important to get new customers because some of your customers will always disappear for various reasons. Some will leave you because they do not need your products and services any longer, companies cease to exist, customers may die, and some simply are dissatisfied with your services. Furthermore, there are limits to the growth in revenue that you can get from your existing customer base, although there are opportunities that you have not thought of, as we will show you a little later in the book.

So what is required to attract and acquire new customers?

o   You need a list of potential customers—or prospects as we normally call them
o   You need to select the prospects that you will prioritize in your pursuit of new customers
o   You need robust and attractive products and service propositions.
o   Attractive functions for the manufactured product and value-adding services for service deliveries
o   You need the right distribution channels
o   You need efficient promotional programs
o   The price must be perceived as reasonable in relation to the performance of what you are delivering
o   You must have some knowledge of who your new customers are
o   The reputation of your products and the associated service quality must be good
o   Your customers must perceive that they have a need for what we offer

o In addition to the functional appeal of the product, you also need some emotional value like prestige, image, design etc.
o Your employees—notably those that are facing the customers—need to believe in what they are promoting

Many of these points are also important in order to retain your existing customers.

The characteristics of these prerequisites are that their efficiency is not very well known since the customers have never been exposed to your products and services before. Of course you normally have some experience from previous attempts to sell the products, which you should capitalize on—but because of these unknowns you get the situation that I stated regarding the cost of acquiring a new customer versus retaining an existing one. Therefore, when you have acquired a customer you should use all means to retain him/her. This is also going to be addressed below.

Develop profitable customers

To develop a customer might sound like a strange expression. However, this is what you should start to do as soon as you have sent the first invoice. The former head of Honda was asked: "*What does it mean to develop the customer?* He answered: "*To sell a car to a customer for the first time is not very difficult. What is difficult is to sell him our brand for the second time.*" You develop a customer through dialogue, contact, service experiences and a flawless product in order to make him repeat his purchase of your brand the next time he is due to acquire a new car and to get him to make purchases of other products that you are offering. This means that you have to create a loyal attitude towards your firm and your products in his mind through the many "moments of truth" that he will have.

• If we start looking at the product that he just bought from you, it is very important that it in all ways matches the expectations that you have created through your promotion—i.e. advertisements in newspapers and magazines, commercials on TV, radio advertisements, billboards, arguments from sales representatives, editorial material that he might have read about you and your products, presentations etc.

- You also have to live up to the service expectations that were formed in the formerly mentioned promotional material. This means that calls to your service center have to be answered promptly; the service representatives that respond to the calls must be well acquainted with the products and services so that the customer feels that he had a useful conversation with your people or agents. The same applies to written communication that should be answered as quickly as possible. That means within a few days when we talk about regular letters and a much shorter time when the customer has contacted you via e-mail. If it will take some time to respond you should always—and I stress always—send him/her a letter or message acknowledging receipt of the inquiry and indicate when he/she can expect an answer.
- The product must also function according to what you have told the customer.

If you let him down on these points, he will be dissatisfied and in the worst case he might find another supplier the next time he is ordering similar types of products and services. He may also start to spread negative information about your company and your products.

Additionally, you will want him/her to extend the range of products and services that he/she buys from you. What you do is to use the knowledge of your customers based on the initial relationship and try to sell him new products and services. This is what we call cross-sale. Here you have a few examples:

- A very obvious thing is for an IT-company to sign a technical service agreement that means that every time there is something wrong with the computer a technician or service representative comes and changes malfunctioning parts or whatever is required to make the machine function again.
- Another example could be a car dealer who wants his garage to take care of all the regular service calls that he has to make including buying spare parts. He will want you to buy extra equipment like a ski box, seat covers, an upgraded radio and CD-player, a car telephone, various electronic articles etc.
- A finance conglomerate that sells all types of financial services and products might want their banking customers to buy additional financial services like loans, insurance packages, funds, stocks etc.,to mention a few.

To do this efficiently you could search for information in the customer database in connection with his previous purchases. Correctly built and with a proper catch of data, your customer base will be an invaluable source of important information about your customers. You might find out a likely profile for the buyers of the other products and services and then direct your promotion towards these types of customers. A smart thing that I have seen when ordering books, videos, DVD's etc. from Amazon—is that they tell what other products and titles that previous buyers of what you are ordering have bought.

The better relationship you are able to create with your customer the more he or she is "dependent" on your company. This means that it will be difficult for him/her to find a new vendor and leave you. He has become dependent on you and it will be costly to leave you. This is particularly the case where there are systems involved that are interfacing with your systems.

The more relationships that you have with your cusomter, the more you can communicate with her in different contexts and make her a loyal customer. Let's look at what happened to my telecommunications need. In the past I only had a regular phone-subscription with my phone company. Today, my family is their customer for regular telephone-services, my wife and I have two mobile telephone subscriptions, this company provides our internet services as well as cable-TV and I also have a fax service that they deliver. This gives this company a vast opportunity to tie me up as a loyal customer and to sell me new things through cross-sales, discount schemes and other marketing activities. The revenue that I pay this company to-day is, of course, far greater than what I paid in the past.

Customer Relationship Management, or CRM, is what we call this type of approach. This is becoming a "buzz"-word in businesses around the globe and what it entails proves to be a valuable approach in improving the relationship with your customers. First of all it is a question of systems—systems that make it possible to administer your client base. Not only **administratively,** i.e. with names, addresses and telephone numbers, but also **statistically** so that you at any given time know what each customer has bought from you, when he bought it from you, if there have been any complaints, if he is reducing the volumes that he is buying from you and many other important facts. However, CRM is also a matter of **philosophy** that creates some rules for how to handle the customers during their lifespan with you. F. ex. what is going to happen if a customer with a certain level of purchasing in the past suddenly has a drop in the business that he is doing with you? What are you going to do when there is a new competitive product on the market? How do you introduce your own product enhancements, new products etc? In other words, based on your own changes and the behavior of your customers, you must act and act in accordance with some predetermined rules. This is what I mean by the serious word philosophy.

Retain profitable customers

The purpose of the development activities that are described above is to retain your customers as long as you want. As you understand retain means to develop customers so that there is a barrier to breaking the relationship with you. To retain customers is also a result of differentiation in the way that you handle your customers. To differentiate means that you also need to have the tools that are required to observe that the customers are different. There are a number of great CRM systems that can provide you with the information that is required to understand differences and also to differentiate. One very important thing is that you understand who your best customers are—in terms of revenue, but equally important in terms of profitability and future potential. Very often it turns out that the most profitable customers are not necessarily your biggest customers. Based on these types of analyses, you can then act as you see fit in the various situations.

Let me give you an example of the way that you could divide your customers into groups based on revenue, and give you some sketchy ideas of how you can handle the customers in the various categories. As a picture to provide you with easy access to my viewpoints, I separate the customers into groups like the airlines use when they differentiate their customers.

- **"Gold Card"** customers are those who should be subject to a very personal customer care program. Normally, although they represent a small part of the total number of customers, they stand for a very large part of the total revenue. In other words it is quite crucial if you should lose these customers. In order to reduce the risk of losing these customers you should give them VIP treatment—which is not wining and dining them as many believe. These customers should have top attention from management and there should be an account plan describing how you want to develop them in terms of revenue increase, new products, strategies, partnerships etc. A member of top management should have the special responsibility of looking after each of the customers in this category. Each year the president of the company should have a personal meeting with the management of the customer to understand the customer's needs, their perception of the relationship and other matters that are of importance for retaining them as a customer. In SAS we said that these customers should be treated with "high touch"—in other words very personally.

- **"Silver Card"** customers are of lesser importance short term—but one of the objectives should be to develop plans for how you could move them into the "Gold Card" category". Although they will not get the same attention as the "Gold Card" customers, there should be much personal contact between them and the management of your company. In regard to management, I do not necessarily mean the top management group, but what you should do is involve management at a lower level. The role of management in this context is to second the sales representatives and demonstrate for the customers that they appreciated his business and that you hold all doors open for them in your pursuit of maintaining them as a customer in the long term perspective and thus help the customer realize his goals and be successful. Many of these customers will have a potential for moving into the "Gold Card" category and you should also have account plans for these that insure that you at least get all their business when they require goods and services that you deliver.

- **"Blue Card"** customers are the huge group of small customers that in numbers are significant, but insignificant as far as contribution to revenue and profit. In SAS we said that these customers should be handled with a "high tech" approach. This meant that their transactions had to be handled very efficiently—mainly by technology and with very limited personal attention. This means that you should try to have them ordering on the web—in other words no telephones, no letters and no faxes that would require manual order entry on your side. Personal customer contact should be through a Call Center and not through a personal representative. Payment should be made through direct debiting or through a purchasing card which would eliminate your risk of having to spend resources on collections and other types of administrative tasks. I am not implying that you should discriminate these customers, but you have to make sure that they give you a positive contribution to your profit in the long run. "In the long run" means that you have to trade off today's low profit (if that is the case) with the long-term opportunities that such customers may represent. These customers normally pay good unit prices, because they are not entitled to the discounts that the bigger customers get. On the other hand, the administrative costs that the handling of them incurs are high because it very often takes the same effort to enter, process, bill and collect an order for a low volume order as it takes for a high volume order.

You should also evaluate whether these small customers are being best handled through you. Maybe there is another distribution channel that could serve them in a more profitable way and provide more service than what you are geared to do. Your upside of this could be to partner with somebody that would pay you a finder's fee or a commission for referring new customers to them—customers that you are not able to serve profitably.

- In addition to these categories you should also focus on a group that we could call **competitive win-backs**. Here you find the customers that you have lost to competition in the past and that are so important that you want to win them back. For this you have to establish special programs. Before you start to design programs you should go through a **loss review** where you identify the main reasons for the loss. When these reasons are "on the table" you have a solid platform for understanding the loss. With this platform it will be much easier to determine what kind of actions you should initiate in order to win the lost customers back. My experience is that there is little focus on this opportunity and not sufficient analysis of what the reasons were for losing the long-term relationship.

Let me show you a live example of what I have tried to demonstrate above. These are some findings that I made in a company that I was a consultant for some time ago.

Analysis of the ABC Results (000NOK)								
Revenue Brackets	Number of customers	Revenue NOK	Gross Margin NOK	Gross Margin % of rev.	ABC cost NOK	ABC cost % of rev.	ABC result NOK	ABC result % of rev.
NOK = USD 0,20								
under 10 000	643	2 387	1081	45,3 %	1652	69,2 %	(571)	-23,9 %
% of total	41,4 %	1,4 %	1,9 %		6,1 %		-2,0 %	
10-50 000	457	10 967	4861	44,3 %	2964	27,0 %	1 897	17,3 %
% of total	29,4 %	6,5 %	8,7 %		10,9 %		6,6 %	
50 - 100 000	154	10 843	4268	39,4 %	2231	20,6 %	2 037	18,8 %
% of total	9,9 %	6,4 %	7,6 %		8,2 %		7,1 %	
100 - 500 000	234	50 734	18070	35,6 %	8249	16,3 %	9 821	19,4 %
% of total	15,1 %	29,9 %	32,3 %		30,2 %		34,2 %	
500 - 1 000 000	32	23 425	7765	33,1 %	3337	14,2 %	4 428	18,9 %
% of total	2,1 %	13,8 %	13,9 %		12,2 %		15,4 %	
1 000 - 2 000 000	18	25 709	7579	29,5 %	3210	12,5 %	4 369	17,0 %
% of total	1,2 %	15,1 %	13,5 %		11,8 %		15,2 %	
2 000 000 and up	14	45 695	12358	27,0 %	5659	12,4 %	6 699	14,7 %
% of total	0,9 %	26,9 %	22,1 %		20,7 %		23,4 %	
Total	1 552	169 760	55 982	100,0 %	27 302	48,8 %	28680	16,9 %
	100,0 %	100,0 %	100,0 %		100,0 %		100,0 %	
Average/customer		109 381	36 071	33,0 %	17 591	16,1 %	18479	16,9 %

This company has 1552 customers. 643 of them have a revenue that is below NOK 10.000. They are making a so-called ABC analysis where they start with the revenue and deduct the cost of goods sold to get the gross margin (GM). From the Gross Margin they take away the ABC cost, which is the cost of handling each order from order entry to billing and collection. This table shows very clearly that the ABC cost for the small customers is a much higher percentage of the revenue than the same cost for the biggest customer. In fact, it is so high that the ABC result for these customers is negative. Furthermore it shows that the customers in the middle of the pack are the most profitable in terms of ABC-result because the combination of gross margin and ABC cost gives the best ABC cost as a percent of revenue.

In addition, the table above shows that:

- **64 customers had revenue above NOK 500.000.** They represent

    o   4% of the total number of customers
    o   56% of the total revenue
    o   49% of the gross margin
    o   45% of the ABC cost
    o   34% of the ABC result
    o   The ABC profitability was 16,9%

If this segment had the same ABC result as the most profitable segment, the result would be increased by 2,7 million.

- The most profitable customers are those **234 that have revenue between NOK 100.000 and 500.000.** Their key figures are

    o   15% of the total number of customers
    o   30% of the total revenue
    o   32% of the gross margin
    o   30% of the ABC cost
    o   34% of the ABC result
    o   The ABC profitability was 19,4%

If all the customers had the same ABC profit % as the customers in this revenue bracket, the result would have been MNOK 4,2 higher.

- Those customers that were billed for **less than NOK 10.000** in year 2000 had these numbers:

    o   41% of the total number of customers
    o   1,4% of the total revenue
    o   1,9% of the total gross margin for the industry segment
    o   6,1% of the ABC cost and
    o   -2,0% of the ABC results
    o   The ABC profitability was minus 23,9%

If this segment had the same ABC result as the most profitable segment, the result would increase by MNOK 1,0 vs. minus MNOK 0.571.

This is a very useful analysis and it was quite a revelation for management when they saw it. I recommended to change the customer care so that "high touch" customer care programs were introduced for the companies in the upper tiers and to introduce "high tech" solutions for the customers in the lower revenue tiers with emphasis on e-commerce and penalties for ordering by phone, fax or letter. It was also recommended that these customers should have a handling fee of about NOK 10 if they did not pay by direct debit or cards.

A particular focus on those customers that have revenue of less than NOK 10.000 per annum shows the following:

The 643 customers in this group had an average revenue of NOK 3.712. We analyzed a random sample of invoices that were issued to 10% of these customers—in total 63 invoices. These 63 invoices had these characteristics:

- Total number of lines   140 (line items)
- Average lines pr. invoice   2,2
- Gross income pr. invoice   NOK 1,492—Total NOK 93.985
- The average discount was   22%
- Net income pr. invoice   NOK 1.159—Total NOK 73.038

User Groups

In many contexts it could also be of significant value to gather your customers—particularly where there are business-to-business relationships—in so-called user groups, where you present news and plans for your products and give your customers a chance to voice their opinions on the products and their relationship with you. Particularly in technology-oriented industries like IT and Telecom, user groups are important tools in the customer communication programs. Through an intelligent monitoring of such events you can get a lot of important information that can be valuable in developing products as well as relationships. In any event you will get positive as well as negative feedback. Since we are not living in a perfect world the negative feedback can be extremely important for you—because it gives you an opportunity to improve in areas where you are not good enough according to your customers. Reacting positively to such input will normally earn you increased loyalty from your customers. And that is what all your customer care programs are aimed at—to make your customers loyal so that they come back and come back and come back.

The table below is an overview of how you can divide your customers into various groups of importance and gives you some idea of the type of customer care programs that you can initiate in order to differentiate the handling of them.

Segmentation of Customers Based on Size of Revenue and previous relationship

Segment terminology	Importance	Attention	Service
VIP-Customers "Gold Cards" 20% of top revenue contributors	Typically 80% of the revenue	Key Accounts served by a dedicated sales force. Annual contact with GM development plan	"High-Touch", very personal service and attention
Solid Customers "Silver Cards" Next 30% revenue contributors with potential to grow	Typically 15% of the revenue	Service approach between Gold Cards and Blue Cards	Cost effective service programs that give the customers a perception of a satisfactory level
Mass Market "Blue Cards" 50% lowest revenue contributors	Many customers, but only a fraction of the total revenue	Impersonalized service Customer contact through e-mail, call center seldom sales - representatives	"High-Tech" mass marketing techniques
Win Backs Lost Gold and Silver card customers the past three years	Often significant contributors to the growth of revenue	Special programs to win back lost customers	"High-Touch", very personal service and attention

I thought I should close this part of the book by quoting a few lines from Oracle's web page where they promote CRM—Customer Relationship Management: *"The key to success is simple—when the relationship to the customer flourishes, your business is flourishing. The closer you are to your customers, the closer you are to success".*

Finance and Administration

What Did Mao Say?

"Have a head for figures." That is to say, we must attend to the quantitative aspects of a situation or problem and make a basic quantitative analysis. Every quality manifests itself in a certain quantity, and without quantity there can be no quality. To this day many of our comrades do not understand that they must attend to the quantitative aspects of things—the basic statistics, the main percentages and the quantitative limits that determine the quality of things. They have no "figures" in their heads and as a result cannot help make mistakes.

"Methods of Work of Party Committees" (March 13, 1949), Selected Works. Vol. IV. p. 379-80. LRB 111.

Place the problems on the table. This should be done not only by the "squad leader", but by the committee memberstoo. Do not talk behind people's backs. Whenever problems arise, place the problem on the table for discussion, take some decisions and the problems will be solved. If problems exist and are not put on the table, they will remain unsolved for a long time and even drag on for years. The "squad leader" and the committee members should show understanding in their relations with each other. Nothing is more important than mutual understanding, support and friendshipbetween the secretary and the committee members, between the Central Committee and its regional bureaus and the area Party Committee.

"Methods of Work of Party Committees" (March 13, 1949), Selected Works. Vol. IV, pp 377-78. LRB 108.

"Exchange information". This means that members of a Party committee should keep each other informed and exchange views on matters that have come to their attention. This is of great importance in achieving a common language. Some fail to do so, and like the people described byLao Tzu, "do not visit each other all their lives, though the crowing of their cocks and the barking of their dogs are within hearing of each other". The result is that they lack a common language.

"Methods of Work of Party Committees" (March 13, 1949), Selected Works. Vol. IV, pp 377-78. LRB 108.

Learn to "play the piano". In playing the piano all ten fingers are in motion; it won't do to move some fingers only and not others. But if all ten fingers press down at once, there is no melody. To produce good music, the ten fingers should move rhythmically and in co-ordination. A Party committee should keep a firm grasp on its central task and at the same time, around the central task, it should unfold the work in other fields. At present, we have to take care of many fields; we must look after the work in all the areas, armed units and departments, and not give our attention to a few problems, to the exclusion of others. Wherever there is a problem, we must put our finger on it, and this is a method we must master. Some play the piano well and some badly, and there is a great difference in the melodies that they produce. Members of the committee must learn to play the piano well.

"Methods of Work of Party Committees" (March 13, 1949),
Selected Works, Vol. IV, pp 379. LRB 110.

Wherever we happen to be, we must treasure our manpower and material resources, and must not take a short view and indulge in wastefulness and extravagance. Wherever we are from the very first year of our work we must bear in mind that many years to come, the protracted war that must be maintained, the counter-offensive, and the work of reconstruction after the enemy's expulsion. On the one hand, never be wasteful and extravagant; on the other actively expand production. Previously, in some places people suffered a great deal because they did not take the long view and neglected economy in manpower and expansion of production. The lesson is there and attention must be called to it.

"We Must Learn to Do Economic Work" (January 10, 1945),
Selected Works, Vol. III, p. 244. LRB185.

Thrift should be the guiding principle in our Government expenditure. It should be made clear to all Government workers that corruption and waste are very great crimes. Our campaign against corruption and waste have already achieved some results, but further efforts are required. Our system of accounting must be guided by the principle of saving every copper for the war effort, for the revolutionary cause and for our economic reconstruction.

"Our Economic Policy" (January 23, 1934),
Selected Works, Vol. I, p. 145. LRB189.

We must see to it that all our cadres and all our people constantly bear in mind that our is a big socialist country but an economically backward and poor one, and that is a very great contradiction. To make China rich and strong need several decades of intense effort, which will include, among other things, the effort to practice strict economy and combat waste i.e., the policy of building up our country through diligence and frugality.

On the Correct Handling of Contradictions Among the People.
(February 27, 1957), 1st pocket ed., p. 71. LRB 186.

We stand for self-reliance. We hope for foreign aid but cannot depend on it; we depend on our own efforts, on the creative power of the whole army and the entire people.

"We Must Learn to Do Economic Work" (January 10,1945),
Selected Works, Vol III, p. 241. LRB 194.

The history of mankind is one of continuous development from the realm of necessity to the realm of freedom. This process is never-ending. In any society in which classes exist class struggle will never end. In classless society the struggle between the new and the old and between truth and falsehood will never end. In the fields of the struggle for production and scientific experiment, mankind makes constant progress and nature undergoes constant change; they never remain at the same level. Therefore, man has constantly to sum up experience and go on discovering, inventing, creating and advancing. Ideas of stagnation, pessimism, inertia and complacency are all wrong. They are wrong because they agree neither with the historical facts of social development over the past million years, not with the historical facts of nature so far known to us (i.e. nature as revealed in the history of celestial bodies, the earth, life and other natural phenomena).

Quoted in "Premier Chou Enlai's Report on the Work of the Government to the First Session of the Third National Peoples' Congress of the People's republic of China" (December 21-22, 1964). LRB 203.

We must learn to do economic work from all who know how, no matter who they are. We must esteem them as teachers, learning from them respectfully and conscientiously. We must not pretend to know when we do not know.

"On the People's Democratic Dictatorship" (June 30, 1949)
Selected Works, Vol. IV, p. 300. LRB 310.

The following is a typical organization for a Finance and Administration function in a company:

The Finance and Administration Department

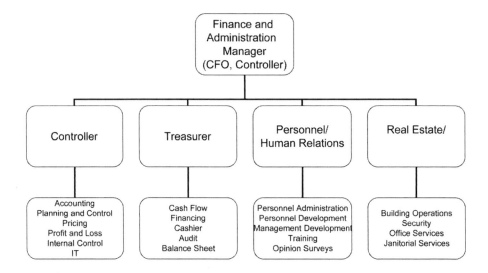

Annual Budgets

The annual budget process is one of the most important processes in a corporation and Chairman Mao stresses the importance of planning in many of his quotations.

In this process you make decisions regarding the forthcoming years of the company, you get a picture of the opportunities of the future, you get some time to think things through together with your management team and for that matter your entire organization. I stress the latter because it is important that your entire organization feels that they own the goals that are inherent in the budget and that they enthusiastically march forward to reach these goals despite the fact that they may be challenging. It is also important that your budget process is based on some formality. This could for instance be:

The planning calendar

This important tool which describes the important days in the process becomes a common reference for all those involved. Typical important events in a budgeting calendar would be:

1. **A kick-off meeting**
   On this date the management of the company should explain the background for the budgeting process, what the most important goals and the challenges are, what strategic decisions have been made that will have an impact on the budget etc. This is an occasion where the management has an opportunity to pump up the staff and ensure their commitment and dedication to the work that lies ahead.

2. **Distribution of assumptions, planning manuals, systems and goals**
   This is the date for the distribution of manuals, guidelines, tools and models etc. that are required to run the process smoothly. In many companies it is normal for top management to communicate what kind of expectations they have to the results that they want to see in the budgets of the operating and staff units. This could be in the form of an absolute profit number, a profit margin, growth in revenue, reduction in cost and expense, improvement in productivity etc.

3. **First submission of the plan document**
   This is the date on which all those who are required to submit input to the budget process have to have their material ready. In a company of a certain size, the Chief Financial Officer consolidates this material into a total plan for the company. If the total of all the partial plans is satisfactory everything is ok. If the result—which is usually the case—is not satisfactory, the company's management will have to determine where they will require more revenue to be generated and less cost and expense to be incurred. This is then communicated to the operating units that are told what portion of the gap between the current plan and the total expectations they are requested to contribute to.

4. **Response to the various organizations**

    Each of the divisions is asked to improve their results through a letter from the group that is responsible for the planning process—normally the Finance Department. The operating units in the company get a certain number of days to assess whether it is possible to make the improvements that they are asked to attain.

5. **Review of the proposed budget**

    At this point in time it is practical to arrange a meeting between the department in question and those who are running the planning process. Often it would be practical for top management to attend this meeting. In this meeting the operating unit has the opportunity to present their plans and their numbers and defend the plan that they have constructed. They will also have the opportunity to tell management why they—if that is the case—are not able to respond positively to the request for improvements.

6. **Final goals**

    In due time before the budget year commences, management communicates the final objectives to the management of the operating units so that they can split the full year budget numbers into Monthly Control Figures—or MCF's as we called them at IBM. The monthly control figures are milestones the company and its operating units should reach as the year proceeds.

7. **Submission of MCF's**

    After the exercise where the operating units have distributed the annual numbers on each of the months of the year, the results are submitted to the central planning unit responsible and consolidated with all the other input.

There are—of course—other ways of running a planning process. The important thing is that you put a structure in place that is suitable to the conditions that prevail in your company.

Assumptions

Since there normally are a number of persons involved in the budget process, it is very important that company management issues guidance and assumptions so that everybody goes in the same direction when the budget work starts. To do this I recommend that management issue a document describing the assumptions that should be borne in mind by everybody. The assumptions could f. ex. contain the following:

- **Macro economic assumptions** like expected inflation, growth in the total economy, foreign currency development, expected macro economic development in the company's most important markets etc.
- **Market assumptions** for our industry like demand predictions, price and supply development for finished goods and production factors like availability of raw materials, semi raw materials, manpower etc. Furthermore, information about the competitive situation, substitute products etc. are valuable.
- The main **overall strategies** and **goals** for the company.
- **Other challenges** that the company may encounter in the next budget period.

Valid and realistic assumptions are of significant importance and will facilitate the budget process, make amendments to the numbers easier, make computations easier etc. Furthermore, it will be easier to defend and explain the budget. Important for these assumptions will be current and past years' experience and external information that you can obtain in the Ministry of Finance, trade associations, on the internet etc.

The Budget Process

Let me in a simple way try to explain how you should run the budget process. There are two important dimensions: One is the **volumes** that the company will produce, generate, sell, hire, rent etc. in order to fulfill its mission. If you do not understand the term volumes now, I hope that it will be clearer as we go along. The other dimension is that there is a unit price attached to these volumes. Hence it is easy to compute the **financial** implications of certain volumes. This is then going into budget. To amend the budget you either change the number of units, the price or both. Let's look more closely at this.

Typical examples of volumes are:

- Units to be sold

    o   If we are a production company, the number of cars, computers, toothbrushes etc. that we are going to sell are units
    o   If we are a consulting company, the unit denomination could be hours, days, weeks, months etc.

- Units to be purchased

    o   Amount of raw material
    o   Number of employees
    o   Number of square meters
        – Office space
        – Production facility space
        – Inventory space
    o   etc.

There are numerous other types of volumes. Each of them has a unit price. These prices are then important for computing the financial implications.

- The input to the **production** process has unit prices like

    o   Raw material pr. kg/liter
    o   Manpower factors like salaries and social expenses

- **Sales**

    o   For each of the products that we are selling there is a unit price. Often there is a gross price from which discounts may be deducted.

- There is a price associated with each **employee**. These are:

    o   Salaries
    o   Social expenses—pension, insurance, cafeteria, contributions to the club
    o   Other expenses like travel, office expenses etc.

- For the **facilities** that we are occupying there will be a unit price for

    o   Rent—number of m²
    o   Energy—number of kwh
    o   Cleaning—price per m²

With all the volumes and their associated unit prices in place we will be in a position to compute the numbers that go into our Profit and Loss statement, our Balance Sheet etc. Let me give you some examples as to how to compute the variables that go into the profit and loss statement:

Description		Type of budgeting unit		Price per budgeting unit
Revenue	=	Expected number of units budgeted to be sold	X	Sales price minus discounts
Cost of Goods Sold	=	Expected number of units to be sold	X	Production cost per unit
Employee Cost	=	Number of employees	X	Average salary per employee
Office Expense	=	Number of employees	X	Average cost per employee
Travel Expense	=	Number of trips to the various destinations * Number of days per trip	X	Ticket price to the various destinations Average meal and hotel costs per day
Finance Cost	=	The amount of bank loans that we have	X	Average interest % on loans
Finance Income	=	The deposits bearing interest that we have	X	Average interest % on deposits
Etc.				

These algorithms are then used to design a computer model that will compute all the numbers required to work out a budget for the following year. There are many ways to present the numbers. One example could be the following:

Profit and Loss – Actual Year 1, Forecast Year 2 and Budget year 3, and Year 4								
	Actual	Forecst	Variance		Budget Year 3		Budget Year 4	
	Year 1	Year 2	Year 2 vs Year 1		MUSD	Yr3/Yr 2	MUSD	Yr4/Yr3
	MUSD	MUSD	MUSD	Index		Index		Index
Total Revenue	9 299	11 220	1 921	121 %	12 300	110 %	13 200	107 %
Cost of goods sold	(4 563)	(5 296)	(733)	116 %	(6 100)	115 %	(6 200)	102 %
% of revenue	-49 %	-50 %	-38 %		-50 %	100 %	-47 %	
Gross Profit	4 736	5 924	1 188	125 %	6 200	105 %	7 000	113 %
% of revenue	51 %	53 %	62 %		50 %	95 %	53 %	
Operating Cost and Expenses	(2 524)	(3 091)	(567)	122 %	(3 385)	110 %	(3 757)	111 %
Of which			(0)		-28 %		-28 %	
Payroll Expenses	(1 612)	(2 002)	(390)	124 %	(2 215)	111 %	(2 395)	108 %
% of revenue	-17 %	-18 %	(0)		-18 %		-18 %	
Depreciation	(275)	(300)	(25)	109 %	(320)	107 %	(350)	109 %
% of revenue	-3 %	-3 %	(0)		-3 %		-3 %	
Other Operating Expenses	(637)	(789)	(152)	124 %	(850)	108 %	(1 012)	119 %
% of revenue	-7 %	-7 %	(0)		-7 %		-8 %	
Operating Profit	2 212	2 833	621	128 %	2 815	99 %	3 243	115 %
% of revenue	24 %	25 %	0		23 %		25 %	
Net Finance	(40)	(120)	(80)	300 %	(92)	77 %	(112)	122 %
% of revenue	0 %	-1 %	(0)		-1 %		-1 %	
Net Before Tax	2 172	2 713	541	125 %	2 723	100 %	3 131	115 %
% of revenue	23 %	24 %	0		22 %		24 %	
Taxes	(270)	(350)	(80)	130 %	(400)	114 %	(456)	114 %
% of revenue	-3 %	-3 %	(0)		-3 %		-3 %	
Net After Tax	1 902	2 363	461	124 %	2 323	98 %	2 675	115 %
% of revenue	20 %	21 %	24 %		19 %		20 %	

Look at all the ratios, percentages and key figures in this chart and compare them to a chart with only absolute figures. Then you realize how poor the chart without these numbers is. In other words—a new demonstration of how useful percentages are.

Monthly Control Figures

In order for us to use the budget as a management tool that facilitates regular monitoring of the results, it is necessary to break down the budget figures into monthly figures, weekly figures, quarterly figures etc. My experience is that in most cases it is most practical to break the numbers into monthly increments. When we do this we establish milestones for where we are going to be during the year in order to reach the annual budget. This distribution on each month of the year can be done in many ways:

- Each yearly figure can be divided by 12
- We can use the distribution that we had last year

- We can use the composite of distributions that we have had for several years
- The annual budget might have been built up so that there is a budget figure per month

Let us see how this is done. In the table below the most important figures from the total full year budget are distributed and the annual figures are broken into 12 increments. In the table you will see that each line item from the budget is being presented four ways:

- In line 1 each annual figure is broken down into a monthly figure
- In line 2 you will find a number that tells how much of each line that will be attained each month expressed in percent
- In line 3 the monthly figures are accumulated so that we also get an impression of how much of the total budget that is supposed to be generated or incurred by a certain month during the year.
- In line 4 you find the accumulated numbers in a given month as a % of the total annual budget.

Monthly Control Figures for Budget Year 2													
	Budget M$	Jan	Feb	Mar	Apr	Mai	Jun	Jul	Aug	Sep	Okt	Nov	Des
Total Revenue	12 300	615	984	984	984	1 230	1 107	738	738	861	1 107	1 353	1 599
Percent per month		5 %	8 %	8 %	8 %	10 %	9 %	6 %	6 %	7 %	9 %	11 %	13 %
Accumulated revenue		615	1 599	2 583	3 567	4 797	5 904	6 642	7 380	8 241	9 348	10 701	12 300
Accumulated percent		5 %	13 %	21 %	29 %	39 %	48 %	54 %	60 %	67 %	76 %	87 %	100 %
Cost of goods sold	(6 100)	305	426	488	426	672	549	366	242	427	549	733	917
Gross Profit	6 200	310	558	496	558	558	558	372	496	434	558	620	682
Percent per month		5 %	9 %	8 %	9 %	9 %	9 %	6 %	8 %	7 %	9 %	10 %	11 %
Accumulated gross profit		310	868	1 364	1 922	2 480	3 038	3 410	3 906	4 340	4 898	5 518	6 200
Accumulated percent		5 %	14 %	22 %	31 %	40 %	49 %	55 %	63 %	70 %	79 %	89 %	100 %
Operating Cost and Expenses	(3 385)	-237	-271	-271	-271	-305	-271	-271	-271	-305	-305	-305	-305
Percent per month		7 %	8 %	8 %	8 %	9 %	8 %	8 %	8 %	9 %	9 %	9 %	9 %
Accumulated cost and exp.		(237)	(508)	(779)	(1 049)	(1 354)	(1 625)	(1 896)	(2 166)	(2 471)	(2 776)	(3 080)	(3 385)
Accumulated percent		7 %	15 %	23 %	31 %	40 %	48 %	56 %	64 %	73 %	82 %	91 %	100 %
Operating Profit	2 815	73	287	225	287	253	287	101	225	129	253	315	377
Percent per month		3 %	10 %	8 %	10 %	9 %	10 %	4 %	8 %	5 %	9 %	11 %	13 %
Accumulated operating profit		73	360	585	873	1 126	1 413	1 514	1 740	1 869	2 122	2 438	2 815
Accumulated percent		3 %	13 %	21 %	31 %	40 %	50 %	54 %	62 %	66 %	75 %	87 %	100 %
Percent of revenue this month		12 %	29 %	23 %	29 %	21 %	26 %	14 %	31 %	15 %	23 %	23 %	24 %
Percent of revenue accumul.		12 %	23 %	23 %	24 %	23 %	24 %	23 %	24 %	23 %	23 %	23 %	23 %

There are many things to observe in this chart. Ideally you should try to schedule your cost & expense lines so that you incur less than 25% as

of March, 50% as of June and 75% as of September of the total annual
budget. As far as revenue items are concerned you should plan to attain
more than 25% in the first quarter, more than 50% by the second quarter
and more than 75% by the third quarter. The result of this is that you
create reserves for the latter part of the year. I admit that this is an ideal
picture and that the real world does not work like this since most companies
have a revenue distribution that is skewed towards the second half and last
quarter of the year.

More follows in the chapter about Management Information Systems.

Cash Flow—Liquidity

There are very few companies that go broke because of bad results—often
the reason that companies go under is that their liquidity is weak or even
negative. The implication of this is that they are not able to pay their bills,
meet their payroll, their taxes or other liabilities. As a consequence it is
of utmost importance that the company has liquidity reserves as well as a
good system of monitoring—plan and manage day by day—the cash flow
development. In addition to securing the necessary funds when liabilities
are due, good cash management provides a return through interest on
funds in the bank and capital gains on investments in stocks or bonds.
However, the latter can also be risky because stock and bond prices can
go up and down. The consequence of this is that the company needs to
develop a cash policy stating how to place the cash—i.e. make a deposit
in the bank, buy shares or bonds, invest in material assets like buildings,
inventories etc.

However—as stressed above—the important thing is that the funds are
invested in objects that can be turned into cash as liabilities are due. "Cash
is king" is a well-known term. There is a lot of truth in this. Let's look at
some of the advantages of good liquidity and negative implications of bad
liquidity—and let me tell you, I have experienced both and there is an ocean
of difference between the two situations.

	Benefits of having an adequate cash flow	Disadvantages with a negative cash flow
Impact on the operations	Facilitates a smooth operation – you get "red carpet treatment" from all your contacts and you do not have the worries that the opposite situation creates.	A difficult cash situation requires the company management to concentrate on a matter that does not bring the company forward. You spend a lot of time on the phone or in meetings with all your creditors instead of looking forward and realizing your visions.
Flexibility	Makes it possible to be opportunistic and take advantage of good offers that might arise as well as realising your short and long term plans.	You are not able to realize your plans and you might renege on promises that you have made earlier.
Cost of credit	The better cash flow, the more advantageous are the financing terms.	The credits needed from banks or other financing institutions become expensive.
Credit-worthiness	Good cash flow creates confidence in the company. You become attractive as a customer: -Suppliers want to give you favorable treatment and create a lasting relationship.	A tight liquidity situation gives a negative reputation, loss of creditworthiness, a need to pay on delivery or in advance for goods and other disadvantages. Banks might be sceptical when you apply for credit and demand all sorts of security and collateral.
The company as an acquisition candidate	The owners can demand a higher price in a sell-out situation when the balance sheet is strong.	A weak cash position reduces the value of the company and it easily becomes inexpensive for investors. Many owners have had to give away a significant share of their ownership for very little money. Many will take advantage of such a weakness.
Employee relations	You might be able to be generous to motivate your employees and give them confidence in the company	Employees might fear bankruptcy and leave the company and the best will leave first – particularly if you start to be late with salary payments.
Customer relations	Your customers stay with you because your company is a going concern that is going to be around in the foreseeable future and is able to develop the business – also to their benefit	Your customers may fear that you might not be around very much longer and seek other vendors of the same type of products and services.
Public relations	A strong balance sheet with a good cash position is something that a financial journalist praises and values	Leads very easily to rumors and gossip and you might spend time defending yourself.

Cash problems hit large as well as small companies. Just as I am writing these lines, I hear on the news that the energy company Enron is in the process of going bust. This was one of the world's largest energy companies with hundreds of thousands of employees. They were not able to pay their bills—so they have had to file for chapter eleven—which in the United States gives them protection from their creditors, while in other countries the procedures might be different. Some time ago we had a similar situation in Norway, where one of the largest and oldest industrial enterprises had problems with liquidity.

The company was managed on a day-by-day basis by the board and the bank as a bankruptcy was initiated and the solution benefitted the man who had capital available to secure continued payments of debt to the creditors. Again, this was a situation where the guy with the cash became king.

These examples were taken from the large corporate world. However, small companies run into problems too. And for them cash management is also a key discipline.

"If your company owes a few hundred thousand, its your problem—if you owe 100 million it's the bank's problem"—a very telling sentence says.

I therefore cannot stress strongly enough that this must have the attention of management to avoid a negative cash position. If you see that you are running into problems as a result of seasonal variances in sales, extraordinary costs or expenses, or something unexpected happening, get in touch with your bank, explain the problem to them, ask them for help. However, do it as early as possible so that they are able to be part of the solution. There is nothing the banks dislike more than a customer who knocks on their door a long time after the fact.

One thing that has struck me is that there are a number of start-ups that raise some money f. ex in an IPO (Initial Public Offering). They establish themselves in the best business districts with beautiful premises, lavish furniture and secretaries here and there. Consequently, they get a tremendous "burn-rate" long before they have invoiced a single cent. "Burn-rate" is a word that was invented during the height of the dot.com boom and defines the number of dollars that were spent per month before the company had come to fruition.

Many of the new companies that went down during the dot.com era incurred a lot more cost and expense than they needed to develop their business idea. I spent some time with a small company trying to start some software activities. They were located on modest premises in the loft of an old building. When their majority stockholder came to the place for a meeting, he was extremely pleased to see the modesty with which the company was run and immediately became motivated for another cash injection. This was an extremely rich, self-made man and he probably thought back on his first days in business with two empty hands. I have learned that management (often young and inexperienced) believed that start-ups required nice premises because that was something that potential customers demanded. This is a grand misunderstanding. Just remember where Bill Gates started *his* activities.

Liquidity sources

There are a number of sources for liquidity like

- **Operations**
  When you have liquidity problems, the cheapest and often easiest way to improve the situation is to better the operational results and fine-tune balance sheet items like accounts payable and accounts receivable. It is the cheapest because it does not cost you interest and other fees. However, it may be easier said than done to reach improvement through improvement in the operations. Let us look at some of the options that you have.

  o   Operational results can be improved through the following:

  ▪   Increase in current and addition of new revenue streams.

  Many companies are giving away product components and service elements that they reasonably could charge for. A regular activity that should be performed by management and employees is a hunt for new revenue streams. F. ex. if the company bills by time units are we certain that we bill all the seconds, minutes, hours that we are entitled to? In a helicopter company I had the following experience. There were varying perceptions among the pilots as to the time the clock started to run when they started a new job. The pilots wanted to be nice to their customers and wanted the clock to start as late as possible. By making a standard rule, which was just a reinforcing of the start time that was specified in the operational manuals, we gained significant revenue that flew straight down to the bottom line. In addition to providing the customers with flight hours we also had a lot of extra equipment that was not part of the standard basis for charging the customers, like lines, baskets, big bags, lifts etc. By starting to charge the customers that had a need for this type of extra equipment we also added to the revenue lines.

- Reduction in cost and expense

  This results—all other things being equal—in higher profits that in turn again result in improved cash flow. Technically, this also ends up as retained earnings in the balance sheet.

o *Accounts Payable—trade creditors*

- If you stretch or renegotiate the payment terms of your vendors or agree to do so with your creditors, you can get a temporary liquidity source

o *Trade debtors*

- As far as Accounts Receivable is concerned, you may enforce a tougher stance regarding payment terms and reminders. Equally—you might change your invoicing schedules compared to what you currently do. Many companies invoice once a month. You can improve the cash flow by daily, weekly, bi-weekly etc. invoicing schedules. You might also be able to get accept for a direct withdrawal from you customers' accounts.
- Factoring—another way of ensuring early payment of your accounts receivable is to sell your dues to a factoring company. This will cost you a fee, but from a total perspective it might be advantageous.

- **Disposal of assets**
  The second step to pursue to improve the cash flow in the company can be to sell assets like buildings, plants, land, machinery, inventories etc. If you dispose entirely of the assets you may lose the opportunity to use the assets to produce revenue that in turn produces profit. However, if there are assets that have no commercial significance for the company this may be a good idea. You may also change the financing of existing assets or finance new assets by means of a leasing arrangement. The former is also called sale and lease back while the latter is either an

operational or financial lease. What you in fact do is you sell the asset to a financing institution and then you lease it back. The lease charge is a combination of the interest level and fees that the financing companies charge as well as the depreciation period for the asset.

- **Owner capital**
  If you were not able to improve your cash flow through the above, the next move would be to approach the owners and ask them for assistance. This is also a cheap way of doing things because you do not pay interest on equity. These are the options that the owners might offer:

  o   Equity

  - Paid-in share capital is an easy way to obtain additional funds and it is cheap because you do not pay any finance charges on equity. In order to get more equity from the owners you must ensure that they have confidence in the company and believe in their long-term prospects.
  - Retained earnings—see dividends below.

  o   Subordinated loans.

    This is a loan normally given by the owners when they do not want to inject more equity. It is normally unsecured; the interests are low and in reality it is very close to equity. The lenders have subordinate status in relationship to the normal debt. If the cash requirement is temporary and the lender does not want to give the cash on a permanent basis, this is a practical way because the loan can be repaid without the legalities that are often required if the cash injection had been equity.

  o   No payment of dividends.

    In a situation where cash is needed for investments or to alleviate a difficult cash situation, the owners may decide at the annual stockholders meeting not to pay a dividend. As a consequence the profits of the company are ploughed back into the company by increasing the retained earning.

- **Banks and Other Financing Institutions**
  They can offer these instruments
  o Regular Loans

    - Short term
    - Long term

  o Drawing Rights
  o Leasing
  o Factoring

- **Restructuring the loan portfolio**
  You may have many loans, in different finance institutions; they may have different terms—down payment and finance charges. If this is the situation, to start negotiations with your bank and reach an agreement to consolidate the picture is normally advantageous. You get fewer loan accounts to monitor and account for. Furthermore, the interest you normally get for the new loan is better than the average for all the small and scattered loans that you had before. In such a situation you might be able to get a repayment period that is longer than the average for the scattered loans that you had before. What you also might get is a window of some months or years where you do not have to repay anything. The only payments that you have to make in this period will be finance charges like interest and fees. In some instances you might get a situation where you pay a small amount back in the beginning and more at the end of the period—like a balloon.

  To create the best climate for this type of negotiations, it is very important to maintain a good relationship with your bank. Make sure that you have regular contact with them, inform them about the situation of your company through calls, meetings and reports. Be frank regarding bad as well as good news. Banks are used to tackling problems—however, what they don't like are surprises that might squeeze them into a corner where their maneuvrability is limited and they are forced to do something which is not consistent with their policies.

- **Conversion of debt to equity**
  A final way of improving your cash position is to agree with your creditors to convert their dues to equity. What it means is that your accounts payable or bank loans are converted to assets for the creditors. The result of this is that your former debt does not burden your financial situation by down payments and finance charges. However, it implies that you get new owners, you may lose control but it might be worth it given the fact that your balance sheet looks stronger and you appear more attractive to the outside.

What you have seen above is a generic list of the alternatives that exist. In real life, solutions may be a combination of the things mentioned above. This is particularly the case when the financing is complicated as it is in large corporations, takes place in various currencies, or comprises a situation with many companies involved. As Chairman Mao and I have stressed many times, it is important to spend time analyzing the situation and making sure that you have the proper tools to do it right.

In order to monitor the cash flow situation you need tools and methods. One important analysis is the Source and Application of Funds Statement that you—in most countries—are obliged to prepare in connection with the year-end closing. This is a snapshot of the situation between the beginning of year and the end of the year and as such is not particularly suited to monitoring the situation on a day-by-day, week-by-week or month-by-month basis. For this, other types of tools are required. In the following I offer a few examples of how this could be done. There are of course a number of ways to do this. The important thing is that you have full knowledge of all your Accounts Receivable and Accounts Payable—the amounts and when they occur. It is very important to be conservative in your estimate—which means do not overestimate your revenue streams and do not underestimate your cost and expenses.

Let us look at some very easy but useful tools for maintaining control over your cash flow.

				Cash In	Cash Out
	December				
				Balance	Balance
Cash position at the beginning of December				250	
Anticipated December movements:					
Payments in					
	November invoices			1 000	
Payments out					
	Salaries				300
	Taxes				150
	Accounts payable				18
	Miscelanneous				80
	Down payment bank loan				28
	Down payment				50
	Down payment tax debt				100
Total transactions				1 000	726
Cash changes for the month of December				274	
Cash position at the end of December				524	

The way you use this simple form is to know the cash position at the beginning of the period (250) and get an overview of all the payments that will occur (1000). For most companies this will be the invoices that are issued for delivery of products and services.
From this all your expected Accounts payable (726) will be deducted. The sum of this (274) is the net cash flow for the month. Remember that the cost and expenses that are booked not necessarily the same as payments out.

				Cash In	Cash Out
	January				
				Balance	Balance
Cash Position at the beginning of January				524	
Anticipated January movements:					
Payments in					
	December invoices			1 044	
	Course revenue			126	
	TVA refund			10	
Payments out					
	Salaries				300
	Taxes				150
	Accounts payable				18
	Miscelanneous				100
	Rent				8
	Overtime payments				1 000
	Down payment bank loan				28
	Interest payment to the bank				100
	Down payment tax debt				100
Total transactions				1 180	1 804
Cash changes for the month of January				(624)	
Cash osition at the end of January				(100)	

During this period there is a negative cash flow (-624) because of heavy payments of expenses that have been accrued during year and down payment of tax debt and bank loan. As a consequence, the cash position at the end of the period is negative (-100). With this in mind the company must start to find solutions for the cash deficit at the end of January. Most companies face cash flow deficits for a period and even a negative cash flow at times. As long as this is seen a long time in advance through a forecasting system, the company can take the necessary steps to cover this when it arises.

		Cash In	Cash Out
February			
		Balance	Balance
Cash Position at the beginning of February		(100)	
Anticipated February Movements:			
Payments in			
January invoices		1 181	
Payments out			
Salaries			350
Taxes			188
Trade creditors			18
Miscelanneous			110
Rent			8
Down payment bank loan			29
Tax debt			50
Down payment government agency			103
Total transactions		1 181	856
Cash changes for the month of February		325	
Cash position at the end of February		225	

This month the cash projection is positive again. The cash change for the month is 325, which gives a cash position at the end of the month of 225. This fact might be enough for the bank to allow a delay in the payment of their loans and make possible similar agreements with other creditors

		Cash In	Cash Out
March			
		Balance	Balance
Cash position at the beginning of March		225	
Anticipated March movements:			
Payments in			
February invoices		1 000	
Payments out			
Salaries			350
Taxes			188
Employer's social contribution			288
Accounts ayable			18
Miscelanneous			60
Rent			8
Down ayment bank loan			29
Down payment tax debt			50
Total Transactions		1 000	991
Cash changes for the month of March		9	
Cash position at the end of March		234	

	Cash In	Cash Out
April		
	Balance	Balance
Cash position at the beginning of April	234	
Anticipated April movements:		
Payments in		
March invoices	1 100	
Payments out		
Salaries		350
Taxes		188
Trade reditors		18
Miscelanneous		110
Rent		8
Down payment bank loan		29
Down payment tax debt		100
Total transactions	1 100	803
Cash changes for the month of April	297	
Cash position at the end of April	531	

Summary of Cash Forecasts					
	December	January	February	March	April
Cash at the beginning of month	250	524	(100)	225	234
Cash in – Accounts receivable	1000	1180	1181	1000	1100
Cash out – Accounts payable	726	1804	856	991	803
Net cash change	274	(624)	325	9	297
Cash at the end of the month	524	(100)	225	234	531

To improve the value of your monthly projections, they should end up in a summary that gives you one total picture for the whole period. Above there is an example of how you can do this. Of course there is a link between the two systems so that if you make changes in the monthly statements this is reflected in the summary statements.

Quality Assurance

What Did Mao Say?

It (a regional or sub-regional bureau of the Central Committee of the Party) should constantly have a grip on the progress of the work, exchange experience and correct mistakes; it should not wait several months, half a year or a year before holding summing-up meetings for a general check-up and correction of mistakes. Waiting leads to great loss, while correcting mistakes as soon as they occur reduces loss.

"On the Policy Concerning Industry and Committee" (February 27, 1948) Selected Works, Vol IV, p. 204. LRB 228.

We must learn to look at problems allsidedly, seeing the reverse as well as the obverse side of things. In given conditions, a bad thing can lead to good results and a good thing to bad results.

On the Correct Handling of Contradictions Among the People (February 27, 1917) 1st pocket ed. Pp 66-67. LRB 222.

One-sidedness means thinking in terms of absolutes, that is, a metaphysical approach to problems. In the appraisal of our work, it is one-sided to regard everything either as all positive or as all negative . . . To regard everything as positive is to see only the good and not the bad, and to tolerate only praise and no criticism. To talk as though our work is good in every respect is at variance with the facts. It is not true that that everything is good; there are still shortcomings and mistakes. But neither is it true that everything is bad, and that, too, is at variance with the facts. Here analysis is necessary. To negate everything is to think, without having made any analysis, that nothing has been done well and that the great work of socialist construction, the great struggle in which hundreds of millions of people are participating, is a complete mess with nothing in it worth commending. Although there is a difference between the many people who hold such views and those who are hostile to the socialist system, these views are very mistaken and harmful and can only dishearten people. It is wrong to appraise work either from the viewpoint that everything is positive, or from the viewpoint that everything is negative.

Speech at the Chinese Communist Party's National Conference on Propaganda Work (March 12, 1957) 1st pocket ed., pp. 16-17. LRB 219.

> *To take such an attitude is to seek truth from facts. "Facts" are all the things that exist objectively, "truth" means their internal relations, that is, the laws governing them, and "to seek" means to study. We should proceed from the actual conditions inside and outside this country, the province, country or district, and derive from them, as our guide to action, laws which are inherent in them and not imaginary, that is, we should find the internal relations of the events occurring around us. And in order to do that we must rely not on subjective imagination, not on momentary enthusiasm, not on lifeless books, but on facts that exist objectively; we must appropriate the material in detail and, guided by the general principles of Marxism-Leninism, draw correct conclusions from it.*
>
> "Refom our Study" (May 1941) Selected Works,
> Vol. III. pp.22-23. LRB 231.

It is an illusion to believe that competitive strategies exclusively can be based on price. For the customer it is necessary to adequately cover his expectations and requirements. Among these, quality is important. We are not only talking about the quality of the product or service that we deliver. We are also talking about the quality of the entire relationship between us as a *supplier* and he as a *buyer*. After all, he is paying your own and your employees' paycheck every month. Hence, he is a pretty important person. He is also an illoyal person who does not stick to you in case you are not living up to your promises in advertisements, sales presentations, TV-commercials etc. and his expectations.

Nowadays, most products (hard and soft) are generic in the sense that very few have technological exclusivity. If they have any advantage, usually it does not last very long because many things are easy to copy. It is normally not difficult to acquire the skills and competence required to manufacture a product or render a service. Given this, it is important to develop other rationales and emotional values that make the customer choose us as a supplier and stay loyal as a customer for ages.

Quality is very important among these values. Quality is embedded in a lot of things—not only in the product or services that you are selling, but in the service that surrounds the ordering and delivery of the product—how he can rely upon you, how fast you respond when he tries to contact you, what kind of reputation that you have, your financial situation, the company's attitude and business practices to mention a few. Therefore it is essential that you monitor your company's quality through policies, objectives, measurements etc. and that you have a system for rectifying situations that are not satisfactory. Since quality is something that everybody contributes to, it is necessary to instill a quality attitude in your organization. My recommendation is that you involve your employees to define how your customers and other stakeholders should perceive you as a quality supplier. One thing I did when I managed a helicopter company was to ask groups of employees like the pilots, the mechanics, the traffic department, the accounting department and other groups of employees what they believed was important to emphasize to secure that the customers perceived us as a quality helicopter operator. Technically, I did this in brainstorming sessions with each of the groups of employees that I mentioned above.

In the brainstorming session the employees were asked to give their opinions on the following questions:

What is important for us to do

- *Before,*
- *during and*
- *after*

a customer assignment so that he/she perceives us as an excellent service provider.

During the brainstorming we filled in the following form:

What do we have to do and how do we have to perform		
Before	**During**	**After**
a customer assignment so that we are perceived to be an <u>excellent</u> service provider so that the customer comes back and back and back............. and spreads the word about our performance?		
Fill in Bullett points ·A ·Etc.	Fill in Bullett points ·B ·Etc.	Fill in Bullett points ·C ·Etc.

In line with the rules for brainstorming, we focused on each of these intervals at a time. Why is *before, during* and *after* so important? The reason for this is the fact that the customer experiences "moments of truth" several times during these intervals. After having brainstormed in several groups, we got a lot of alternatives. Then we again solicited the assistance of all the employees. We gave them all the alternatives that had come up during the brainstorming session and asked them to identify the top five in each category. Based on the opinions of the employees we were able to rank the seven most important things do to under each category. The results are found in the table below. With this table in hand we started to "indoctrinate" all the employees and we made this our service promise to the customers. Whenever we had customer sales presentations we showed them this table.

Let me briefly explain to you what kind of business this was. Inland helicopter flying is transportation of personnel and cargo. In Norway it normally takes place in remote areas where land transportation is difficult and helicopters are the only "transportation horse" when things are being transported into the mountains. The customers were construction companies that were building dams, power plants that needed helicopters for inspection of the snow-depth and other things that power production is dependent on. An important type of mission was to fly materials into the bush for construction of power transmission lines. Once in a while the mission was to fly hunters into the deserted mountains to hunt reindeer and other wild animals. One characteristic of the business was that there was a very short time lag between the order and the execution of the job—normally just a couple of days. Consequently, the order backlog was very short. These were the circumstances of this company and of course they are impacting the content of the three columns. Search and Rescue as well as ambulance helicopter services were other types of missions that the company was engaged in.

The next step was to get "buy-in" or acceptance from the employees. After this acceptance, the employees were asked to put life into each of the statements by brainstorming around what specific things that their group should do in order to create the customer perception that was the aim of the exercise.

What we have to do and how we have to perform		
Before the mission	During the mission	After the mission
so that the customer perceives us as an <u>excellent</u> service provider?		
·Be available 24 hours a day, 7 days a week, 365 days a year ·Always give the customer the impression that we value him highly ·Help the customer define his needs through information inquiry ·Give the customer information about what is going to happen, where it is going to happen and when it is going to happen ·Give the customer a single point of contact ·Be punctual and always inform the customer well in advance when we are late ·Ensure that the right type of helicopters and auxiliary equipment are present before we fly to the customer meeting point	·Ensure that the pilot and co-pilot are sufficiently skilled to accomplish the mission ·Meet the customers with presentable aircraft and personnel ·Brief the customer at the site of the mission about what is going to happen and what is important for safety purposes ·Accomplish the mission in a safe way without taking chances ·Deliver as agreed and promised ·Communicate consistently so that the crew says the same thing as the Traffic Department ·Create an atmosphere of calmness, safety and precision that is imposed on the customer and other involved parties	·Terminate the mission in an orderly fashion ·Evaluate the execution together with the customer immediately after the mission is completed ·Assist in cleaning up the landing sites ·Thank the customer for the business and the cooperation before take-off ·Ensure that the invoice contains no surprises and is understandable, correct and issued timely ·Contact the customer some time after the mission is accomplished to listen to his opinion and to give him the impression that we want to have him as a customer again
Always have a friendly, polite and professional attitude		
All employees are responsible for this		

There are two important things that are particularly stressed in this table:

- The importance of precise and frequent communication and
- Safety-oriented matters.

Because of the nature of the helicopter business, these were two extremely important quality elements. A consultant company would have an entirely different focus, as would a manufacturer of furniture, a distributor of building materials, a cinema, a computer manufacturer, a hospital, a grocery store, a telephone company, a bus company, a conference organizer, a travel agency etc. What is important *before*, *under* and *after* the delivery of the product and services therefore varies extremely from company to company and from industry to industry. One thing that is important everywhere, however, is good communication, customer service and professionalism.

Try to do this exercise in your own company. I am sure that you will get some interesting results—results that might compel you to take action that will improve your standing in the eyes of your customers. I believe that you often will be talking about small matters that can easily be rectified.

We might have *our* opinion of what the customer perceives as quality. It might not necessarily correspond exactly with the customers' opinion.

It might, therefore, be useful to let a panel of customers answer the same questions or make a survey among your customers.

If you have not yet done it, start a quality revolution—make sure that all your employees understand his or her role in the creation of a quality perception among the customers. Include your partners like the most important suppliers, transportation companies, dealers and others that are associated with you and impacts the customers' perception of you as far as quality is concerned. Experience shows that companies obsessed with quality thrive in many ways. They become more profitable, their employees become more energized and their customers become more satisfied than what is the case in companies without this emphasis.

The content of such a quality revolution is described in Tom Peters' Book *Thriving in Chaos*. I have paraphrased his words as follows:

- Make sure that management is obsessed with quality and makes it a major focus area and something they are committed to. Do not pay lip service to this but "walk the talk", demonstrate every day that this is high up on your agenda as the top executive and make sure that this is the case for your functional managers also.
- Choose a system to guide you and your employees towards the ultimate. There are many systems described in all the literature that exists about this subject. One can be as good as another. Choose one or design one yourself and follow it religiously.
- You must measure quality. Put in place quality objectives in all areas and measure the performance regularly. Do this in areas that are very visible and in areas that are not in the limelight. Make sure that all your employees have quality objectives in their performance requirements.
- Reward quality achievements. Solicit your employee's support of quality and motivate them through rewards for the continuous achievements of their objectives. Also, distribute ad hoc rewards when warranted. F. ex. each time you receive a letter from a customer that commends an employee for good work, a polite attitude or other evidence of good service recognize this by posting the letter, mentioning it in the company newspaper, sending him a little note etc. Another type of reward is to grant awards for quality inventions

that correspond to a certain portion of the financial benefit that a quality proposal has yielded.

- Give your people quality training. As is said in Japan: "Quality control starts with training and ends in training". Do not train the first and second line managers only, but the top management as well as all the non-managerial staff. Give them regular training in order to keep the "quality torch burning". Make sure that new employees get their first doses of quality indoctrination in the "Fresh employees' introductory". You do not have that? Get it started as quickly as possible if you want as much involvement and productivity as early as possible from the newly employed. Lack of information and involvement among recently hired people are major reasons why people leave during their first year of employment.

- Use cross-functional teams to handle quality problems. Quality issues are not normally confined to one function or area. Therefore it is necessary to address this with people mastering difficult disciplines and responsible for different areas. Remember the people performing operations understand where "the shoe pinches".

- Small is beautiful. Give credit for and recognize small quality improvements.

- Appoint quality champions that are responsible for monitoring quality. Find them among the rank and file people. You will be surprised to see their kind of involvement and dedication and the difference that they will make because they know where the problems are. They will also demonstrate sides of themselves that you did not believe existed and that they were often unaware of themselves.

- Make customers, suppliers, transporters and others strategic quality partners and include them in your quality processes. Agree on quality objectives and meet with them regularly to review progress. Recognize good results and do not hesitate to put problems on the table for discussion.

- Quality improvements increase profit. Costs go down and revenues go up. To do things right the first time avoids extra work, explanations and excuses. For quality products with zero defects you can charge higher prices.

- Insure that there is a constant focus on quality and its importance. In the United States one would use a Quality Badge that has a text that reinforces the quality revolution. Regularly posting quality numbers is another way. The company president should stress its importance when he addresses the employees in speeches and interviews. "Quality is a never-ending story."

Best Practice and Benchmarking

These two terms indicate two of the best ways of understanding how to get inspiration to make improvements and to enhance your performance or operations. Look at comparable businesses that are doing better than yourself, including other companies in your industry and find out what makes them better than you and other operators in the business. When you have determined this you must adapt that knowledge to your own situation—i.e. make organizational changes regarding structure and people, change your production equipment, find new suppliers of raw materials, services and everything else that goes into producing and delivering your product—whether it is goods or services. You should also try to establish a system where you compare your own performance with that of your competitors on a regular basis. Very often trade associations do that as a service to their members. What they often do is analyze the accounting or sales volume figures without revealing the names of the other companies.

Service Level Agreements

When you enter into a relationship with an outside company from which you are going to get a regular delivery of goods or services, you should insist on a service agreement where your expectations to service, quality, lead times, handling of complaints, how you communicate, how you are compensated when there is non-compliance etc., are spelled out. Normally it is more than what is mentioned in the contract or purchase order. From time to time you should also meet with the relevant people in the other organization to review progress and the entire situation. This is important as a buyer of products or services, but also as a supplier. If you go to your customers and tell them that you would like to understand what they expect and that you also would like to record this in a mutually binding agreement, you will cement the relationship between you and your customer in a very positive way.

Deviations

Measurements are an important part of the quality assurance effort of a company. You therefore need to establish quality standards and regularly measure to what extent you meet these standards. If you do not meet them, you have a deviation. A simple way of defining a quality deviation is to say that a deviation is a situation that is different from the situation that you have determined that you want to have. Quality deviations can be measured on a hourly basis, a daily basis, weekly, monthly, or yearly. Each company has to establish the service quality that is relevant to them, monitor them regularly and take action when out of line situation occurs. Let's face it—the future winners in business will be those companies or individuals who live up to their service promises and their customers' expectations.

Management Information Systems

What Did Mao Say?

"Grasp firmly". This is to say, the Party committee must not merely "grasp", but "grasp firmly", its main task. One can get a grip on something only when it is grasped firmly, without the slightest slackening. Not to grasp firmly is not to grasp at all. Naturally, one cannot get a grip on something with an open hand. When the hand is clenched tightly, there is still no grip. Some of our comrades do grip the main tasks, but their grasp is not firm and so they cannot make a success of their work. It will not do to have no grasp at all, nor will it do if the grasp is not firm.

> "Methods of Work of Party Committees" (March 13, 1949).
> Selected Works, Vol. IV. p. 377. LRB 111.

Place the problems on the table. This should be done not only by the "squad leader", but by the committee members too. Do not talk behind people's backs. Whenever problems arise, place the problem on the table for discussion, take some decisions and the problems will be solved. If problems exist and are not put on the table, they will remain unsolved for a long time and even drag on for years. The "squad leader" and the committee members should show understanding in their relations with each other. Nothing is more important than mutual understanding, support and friendship between the the secretary and the committee members, between the Central Committee and between the regional bureau and the area Party Committee.

> "Methods of Work of Party Committees" (March 13, 1949),
> Selected Works. Vol. IV. p. 377. LRB 108.

Learn to "play the piano". In playing the piano all ten fingers are in motion; it won't do to move some fingers only and not others. But if all ten fingers press down at once, there is no melody. To produce good music, the ten fingers should move rhythmically and in co-ordination. A Party committee should keep a firm grasp on its central task and at the same time, around the central task, it should unfold the work in other fields. At present, we have to take care of many fields; we must look after the work in all the areas, armed units and departments, and not give our attention to a few problems, to the exclusion of others. Wherever there is a problem, we must put our finger on it, and this is a method we must master. Some play the piano well and some badly, and there is a great difference in the melodies that they produce. Members of the committee must learn to "play the piano" well.

"Methods of Work of Party Committees" (March 13, 1949).
Selected Works, Vol. IV. p. 379. LRB 110.

"Have a head for figures". That is to say, we must attend to the quantitative aspects of a situation or problem and make a basic quantitative analysis. Every quality manifests itself in a certain quantity, and without quantity there can be no quality. To this day many of our comrades do not understand that they must attend to the quantitative aspects of things—the basic statistics, the main percentages and the quantitative limits that determine the qualities of things. They have no "figures" in their heads and as a result cannot help make mistakes."

"Methods of Work of Party Committees" (March 13, 1949).
Selected Works. Vol. IV. p. 379-80. LRB 111.

The purpose of the Management Information System of a company is among other things what is mentioned in the four quotes above. First of all it should help you and your colleagues in management to grasp firmly what is happening in the business. Another purpose is to get the problems on the table for analysis, discussion, decision and timely action. In these discussions the members of management will often have varying viewpoints depending on the role that they have in the company. Irrespective of these varying roles, it is important to have the type of mutual understanding that Chairman Mao mentions. With mutual understanding my interpretation is that the members of the management group should respect the roles that the others are playing. I like the analogy of "learning to play the piano". It says something about central tasks as well as other fields, putting a finger on the problems and doing something about them and ensuring that the management group work together in harmony.

Irrespective of the size that your business has—you need a monitoring system that ensures that you reach the goals that you have in various areas and that you firmly grasp as much as possible about your business. This applies to a small start-up business as well as to a large corporation. It is the responsibility of the Chief Executive to put in place a system that ensures that

- the organization knows where it is going,
- it is on track,
- it is focussing and
- helps him show leadership.

There are a few other quotes that I also would like to start this section of the book with:

- **"What's measured, gets attention."**

This is an expression that I heard from Jan Carlzon, the former head of Scandinavian Airlines System—whom I had the pleasure to work with for several years during my tenure in this corporation. In other words, if your management group has decided to observe a certain phenomena and present it to each other, let's say every month, you can be certain that whenever you present the figures it will get everybody's attention and be subject for discussion—particularly if there is a negative development. However, the important question is—what to measure? The numbers that we normally measure are historical data from the books of accounts. This type of information is the same from period to period and governed by the laws of the country in which the company is operating. Although they are very important as a means to assess the past, the question is whether they help management to do a better job. In my opinion, accounting records are mainly suited to give management a confirmation of past performance and only partially suited to determine whether things are going well or not. Another pitfall is that the formats in which the information is given, tends to stay the same for a long time and in many cases it appears as if this information is the same from corporation to corporation.

You have to supplement the measurement of the past with information that tells you if you are successful in implementing your strategy and that the plans and strategies for the future have a likelihood of being carried out. It is therefore important that you—together with your management team and employees—determine what is it that you must measure in order to control regularly that you are heading towards the goals and visions that you have established and that the assumptions for the strategies are still valid. This will of course be individual from company to company, from industry to industry, and from country to country. The size of the companies will also impact the type of performance measures that you determine to use for your business. In well-managed companies the senior management recognizes very well the role of performance measurements. In a later chapter of the book I will be more specific as to the way you should organize your performance measurements.

- **The optimal amount of information**

We are living in the information age, we are being inundated with data, data and information streams towards us and it is very difficult to sort out what is really needed to do our job right. It is important that you as manager select the information that is required for **you** to do the job—otherwise you will be bogged down in so much information that you will be unable to do your job. It is important that you are conscious of this and select what you want on a regular basis and discard what you do not need.

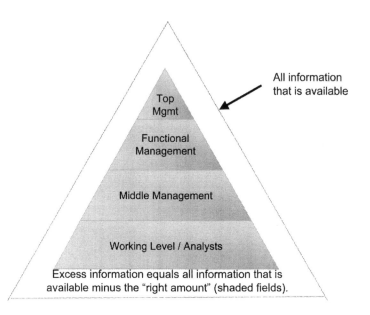

Excess information equals all information that is
available minus the "right amount" (shaded fields).

The relationship between the information that is available and the information that is needed to manage the company is expressed in this figure. The amount of data that is available is depicted by the dotted line, while management at different levels only need what is in the shaded triangle. At all levels one must pick the data that is necessary and skip all the data that is superfluous. This way you get an **information flow that is optimal** to the needs of the company at all levels.

I remember as the president of a company, I received floods of data. In the beginning I tried to relate to all this data, but I soon found out that I had to select the data that I needed to mange the company, to understand what was happening and to be able to take the action required to correct or eradicate unsatisfactory situations. I asked my direct reports to determine what they needed and so forth. Through this exercise. we were able to determine an optimal structure for the MIS (Management Information System) that we wanted to apply to our company.

- **"Turn data into knowledge."**

Most companies have vast amounts of data. However, this data is often not organized in a way that makes them very meaningful or useful in managing the company. Nevertheless, with relatively simple ways of reorganizing the data, you might derive a lot of meaningful information that will enhance your understanding of what is going on. Here are some examples. Let us again view the Income and Expense Statement that you initially saw on pages 81 and 82.

Basic Profit and Loss Data			Year 1	Year 2
Total Revenue			9 299	11 220
Cost of Goods Sold			(4 563)	(5 296)
Gross Profit			4 736	5 924
Operating Cost and Expenses			(2 524)	(3 091)
Of which				
Payroll Expenses			(1 612)	(2 002)
Depreciation			(275)	(300)
Other Operating Expenses			(637)	(789)
Operating Profit			2 212	2 833
Net Finance			(40)	(120)
Net Before Tax			2 172	2 713
Taxes			(270)	(350)
Net After Tax			1 902	2 363

The line items and absolute figure in the two tables are exactly the same. However, as you can see, we have enriched the data in the table on page 82 with percentages and ratios that makes the table much more useful and readable. By adding a few columns such as

- The absolute difference between Year 1 and Year 2
- The relative difference between the same two columns

we get interesting additional information and knowledge because we easily see if there has been an increase or a decrease in the different line items from year to year.

By computing the ratios—relationships—between the various "negative" line items such as cost of goods sold, the various expense items etc. and the revenue, we get an indication of the "quality" of the numbers each year and how the "quality" is changing from year to year, from period to period,

company to company, department to department etc. The legibility of the
chart also increases by use of colors, bold face type etc. With the modern tools
that are now available, there are an abundance of methods and techniques
that you can use to make your data tables and graphs more informative than
could be done in the past.

Enriched Profit & Loss Figures						
			Year 1	Year 2	Year 2/Year 1	
			MUSD	MUSD	MUSD	Index
Total Revenue			9 299	11 220	1 921	120,7 %
Cost of Goods Sold			(4 563)	(5 296)	(733)	116,1 %
% of revenue			-49,1 %	-47,2 %	1,9 %	
Gross Profit			4 736	5 924	1 188	125,1 %
% of revenue			50,9 %	52,8 %	1,9 %	
Operating Cost and Expenses			(2 524)	(3 091)	-567	122,5 %
% of revenue			-27,1 %	-27,5 %	-0,4 %	
Of which						
Payroll Expenses			(1 612)	(2 002)	(390)	124,2 %
% of revenue			-17,3 %	-17,8 %	-0,5 %	
Depreciation			(275)	(300)	(25)	109,1 %
% of revenue			-3,0 %	-2,7 %	0,3 %	
Other Operating Expenses			(637)	(789)	(152)	123,9 %
% of revenue			-6,9 %	-7,0 %	-0,2 %	
Operating Profit			2 212	2 833	621	128,1 %
% of revenue			23,8 %	25,2 %	1,5 %	
Net Finance			-40	-120	-80	300,0 %
% of revenue			-0,4 %	-1,1 %	-0,6 %	
Net Before Tax			2 172	2 713	541	124,9 %
% of revenue			23,4 %	24,2 %	0,8 %	
Taxes			(270)	(350)	(80)	129,6 %
% of revenue			-2,9 %	-3,1 %	-0,2 %	

At the bottom we get a very important ratio—the profit ratio. This ratio
shows how many dollars the company has in profit or loss for each revenue
dollars that they have billed. This is the ratio that is mostly focused on.
However, it is equally important to look at the other ratios. For instance, if
the Net After Tax to Revenue deteriorates, you can start to determine the
reasons by analysing why the net profit ratio is not developing as it should.
This you can do in a **margin analysis** that is an extract of the information
that you find in the table below:

		Year 1	Year 2	Variance
Margin Analysis				
Total Revenue		100,0 %	100,0 %	
Cost of goods sold		-49,1 %	-47,2 %	1,9 %
Gross Profit		50,9 %	52,8 %	1,9 %
Operating Cost and Expenses		-27,1 %	-27,5 %	-0,4 %
Of which				
Payroll Expenses		-17,3 %	-17,8 %	-0,5 %
Depreciation		-3,0 %	-2,7 %	0,3 %
Other Operating Expenses		-6,9 %	-7,0 %	-0,2 %
Operating Profit		23,8 %	25,2 %	1,5 %
Net Finance		-2,1 %	-1,1 %	1,0 %
Net Before Tax		23,4 %	24,2 %	0,8 %
Taxes		-2,9 %	-3,1 %	-0,2 %

From this you can see that the Net Before Tax as a percent of revenue has improved by 0.6 points in 2005 compared to 2004. The reason for this is a combination of
• an improved Gross Profit Margin because of a lower Cost of Goods Sold ratio than in the former year,
• the Operating Cost and Expense Ratio has *deteriorated* by 0.4 pts. due to small changes in the relationship of payroll, depreciation and other operating expenses to revenue.
• Furthermore, there has been a *negative* development in the Net Finance Cost to revenue relationship.
The next step in the analysis is to find out why the relationships have developed as shown in this table.

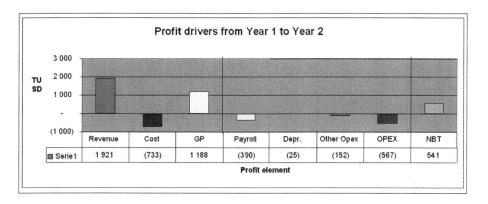

If you want to see graphically the factors have driven the profit the profit from what it was in year 1 to year 2, you can construct a graph of the type that is called "Profit Drivers from Year 1 to Year 2". Each column represents the most important line items in the Profit and Loss Statement. Those that point up show where the positive impact has come from and those that point down represent those with a negative impact on the profit from year to year.

I am certain that you will agree with me when I contend that the 2 previous tables and the graph are far more informative than the table that contained absolute numbers only. And remember the basic information—the absolute figures are exactly the same in both. I will again stress the following quotation from Chairman Mao's works:

> *"Have a head for figures. That is to say, we must attend to the quantitative aspects of a situation or problem and make a basic quantitative analysis. Every quality manifests itself in a certain quantity, and without quantity there can be no quality. To this day many of our*

comrades do not understand that they must attend to the quantitative aspects of things—the basic statistics, the main percentages and the quantitative limits that determine the quality of things. They have no "figures" in their heads and as a result cannot help make mistakes."

The more I read these few lines the happier I become with Chairman Mao's works as a guide for business managers.

The table below is another example of "live" data from a company situation where the raw data has been enriched through data organization and use of percentages. The basis for this table was a data file with the revenue per customer in a certain year. The raw data list expressed very little, but when it was turned into a table that fits into less than one page, it became very legible for management. The data was turned into knowledge by means of a table that reveals a lot of extremely important information for company management. Let's look at it:

Analysis of Customer Activity									
	Number of Customers				Sales				
Sales Brackets	Absolute numbers		Percent		Average	Total		Percent	
NOK 000	Per	Accu-	Per	Accu-	Per	This	Accu-	This	Accu-
NOK = USD 0.20	category	mulated	category	mulated	customer	Line	mulated	Line	mulated
More than 10 milion	1	1	0,1 %	0,1 %	15 806	15 806	15 806	8,9 %	8,9 %
5 – 10 milion	4	5	0,2 %	0,3 %	5 924	23 696	39 502	13,4 %	22,3 %
1 – 5 milion	27	32	1,6 %	1,9 %	2 099	56 673	96 175	32,1 %	54,4 %
500 000 – 1 milion	34	66	2,0 %	3,9 %	747	25 398	121 573	14,4 %	68,8 %
100 000 – 500 000	156	222	9,2 %	13,1 %	214	33 384	154 957	18,9 %	87,7 %
50 000 – 100 000	142	364	8,4 %	21,4 %	69	9 798	164 755	5,5 %	93,2 %
10 000 – 50 000	399	763	23,5 %	45,0 %	24	9 576	174 331	5,4 %	98,6 %
1 – 10 000	605	1 368	35,7 %	80,6 %	4	2 420	176 751	1,4 %	100,0 %
No sales in that year	329	1 697	19,4 %	100,0 %	-	-	176 751		
Total	1 697		100,0 %		104	176 751			

The table is constructed as follows:

- The customers are broken down in various revenue brackets—column 1.

- There is one main section for the number of customers and for the sales to these customers.
- In each of these two main sections there is one column showing the number for this line item (per category) and one that shows the accumulated number. Example: There is one customer in the revenue bracket with more than NOK 10 mill in revenue, while there are 4 in the bracket between NOK 5 and 10 mill. Hence, the accumulated number of customers is five and so forth.
- The same applies to the sales section, where in addition the first column shows the average revenue for the customers in the various brackets.

There are a number of very interesting observations to be made by reading this table. Let me give you some examples.

1. Five customers—0,2% of the total number of customers stand for a total revenue of NOK 39,5 mill. or 22,3% of the total revenue
2. There were 66 customers with a revenue of more than NOK 500.000.

   - They represent 3,9% of the total number of customers and
   - Stand for 68,8% of the total revenue

3. 19,4% of the customers that had revenue in the previous year had no revenue in the current year. If I were the sales director, I would be extremely interested in knowing why.
4. 605 customers—35,7% of the total number of customers—had revenue of NOK 2,2 mill which is 1,3% of the total revenue. The average for these customers was NOK 4.000. Here I would be very interested in understanding whether these customers were profitable at all.
5. The mean customer had a revenue of only NOK 10.000.

Please try to make other observations and conclusions based on this table yourself and ask questions that you would pose if you were the General Manager or a member of the management group of this company.

I hope this very well describes how you convert data to knowledge and understanding—knowledge and understanding that is actionable. The revelations of this table led to the construction of the table that you see on page 126. A "Gold Card" customer care program was made for the most valuable customers and a "Blue Card" for the customers with revenues of less than NOK 10.000. We also identified a need for a "Win Back" program for customers that we had lost the past year.

As you have seen many places in Mao's quotations, he stresses the need for making analyses to have a firm grasp of the realities. Do the same analysis based on your own customer base. I am certain that you will find some staggering facts that will make you understand your own business better and that you will call for action that suits the particular situation that you are in.

Where are we going?

I recommend that your company establish a Management-by-Objectives philosophy. These are descriptions of goals that should be reached within a certain time period. These objectives should of course support the attainment of the overall company goals and objectives. They should be stated in a written document that can be considered a type of "contract" between employees and their managers at all levels of the organization. I stress "all levels".

It is the responsibility of the CEO to make this clear and to establish overall operational objectives that clearly show where you are headed. These overall objectives should then be broken down in divisional objectives. The divisional objectives are broken down in departmental objectives and the departmental objectives are broken down into individual objectives. This hierarchy can be illustrated by the following figure:

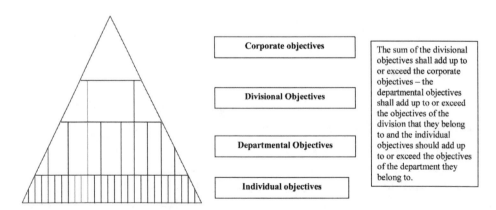

Corporate objectives

Divisional Objectives

Departmental Objectives

Individual objectives

The sum of the divisional objectives shall add up to or exceed the corporate objectives – the departmental objectives shall add up to or exceed the objectives of the division that they belong to and the individual objectives should add up to or exceed the objectives of the department they belong to.

It is very important that the objectives are operational. They should therefore be

- Measurable, addressing elements like quantity, quality and time
- Challenging but realistic
- Fair
- Known and accepted by the receiver
- Oriented towards activities and results
- Relevant for the persons who receive them
- Constructed so that they can be impacted by the receiver

Performance Reviews

An important part of he Management Information System is the frequency with which you receive and review the results and can make observations. Given the business you are in and the part of the business that is in focus, the frequencies with which you monitor the various aspects could be hourly, daily, weekly, monthly, quarterly, bi-yearly, yearly, etc.

The frequency will also depend on what is practical, the competitive situation, the phenomena that you want to observe, legal requirements, the level in the organization that is responsible for corrective actions in case there are deviations, how fast you can generate information etc. However, there always has to be a trade-off between the speed of securing the information and processing them and the cost associated with doing this.

It is important that the material is presented in a way that makes it readable. It should contain quantitative as well as qualitative information—information that is compared to standards, budgets, norms, past periods and from which you can draw conclusions and take corrective action and determine where responsibilities lie.

Since there is such a variety of businesses and different conditions it is difficult to give examples, but as a general rule such information has to be generated in the following areas:

o   Financial Planning and Control
o   Production—Efficiency and Quality
o   Procurement
o   Quality

o   Customer Satisfaction
o   Market Situation
o   Employee Satisfaction
o   Competitive activity

You need to initiate a process whereby your managers and employees help you to identify the kind of observations that are required to manage and monitor your business in an optimal way.

In what direction are you looking?

Most of the information that is evaluated in the performance reviews is **historical**. Past performance is what we mostly measure because that is very often the easiest. These consist of sales records, accounting records like the Profit and Loss Statements and the Balance Sheets and the Capacity Utilisation Report. However, it is equally important to have a **forward-looking** approach as well. One of the first things that I became acquainted with as a young trainee at IBM, was the order backlog. This is one of the most useful forward-looking tools that you have. The order backlog tells you many important things that help you monitor the business in the months to come. First of all, it gives you a good indication of the revenue that you will generate in the next couple of months and indicates to you if you are on the way to deviating from your budget, what types and amounts of raw material that you need, and what capacity you need to transport the finished goods to your customers. If your backlog is not living up to expectations, there is a need for corrective action. There are many ways of reporting and presenting the order backlog situation. Let me give you one example.

The company in the example below is selling technical manpower services to the oil industry in the North Sea on the south-western coast of Norway and the eastern coast of the United Kingdom. The industry is very volatile because the activity level is dependent on the oil prices and the weather conditions. Since the weather conditions are very bad during the winter, there is normally a low activity level during the months of November, December, January and February. It is therefore necessary to make sure that the spring, summer and early fall months are filled with activity to compensate for the quiet periods during the winter. In addition to the main activity, the company also offers training courses.

There was absolutely no control of how the orders matched the budgets. Hence, there was no system in place to tell management that they had to increase their marketing activity when things were slower than desirable.

To get this under control we designed the very simple chart below. Before we look at the form, I would like to stress that all data required to generate the analysis was in place. Thus, these simple tools should have been in place by management's own imagination long before my management-consulting firm came into the picture.

Result and Forecast for Manpower Services and Training Courses									
	Legend	Result +	Budget	vs. monthly budget		2	3	4	5
TMOK	NOK=0.2 USD	Backlog		NOK	%				
		A	B	A-B	A/B				
Revenue year to date - July									
Manpower services	1	5 463	5 700	-237	96 %				
Training courses		269	150	119	180 %				
Total revenue yld		5 732	5 850	-118	98 %	+			
Result July + backlog August									
Manpower services	2	1 025	1 050	-25	98 %				
Training courses		125	120	5	104 %				
Total forecast		1 150	1 170	-20	98 %	+			
Revenue yld + backlog		6 882	7 020	-138	98 %	=	+		
Result July + backlog August and September									
Manpower services	3	700	1 050	-350	67 %				
Training courses		137	140	-3	98 %				
Total forecast		837	1 190	-353	70 %		+		
Revenue yld + backlog		7 719	8 210	-491	94 %		=	+	
Result July + backlog August, September and October									
Manpower services	4	740	1 050	-310	70 %				
Training courses		156	133	23	117 %				
Total forecast		896	1 183	-287	76 %			+	
Revenue yld + backlog		8 615	9 393	-778	92 %			=	+
Result July + backlog August, September, October and November/December									
Manpower services	5	2 036	1 900	136	107 %				
Training courses		687	500	187	137 %				
Total forecast		2 723	2400	323	113 %				+
Revenue yld + backlog		11 338	11 793	-455	96 %				=

This is only one of the many ways of analyzing the order backlog situation. The method is as follows (the numbers in front of each of the sentences below refer to the numbers in the table above):

1. These are the revenue results as of the month of July compared to the budgets—absolute and relative figures.
2. The first three lines show the figures from the order backlog for the two revenue sources and total for the month of August. The total of this is added to the July results year-to-date to get the year-to-date August projection.
3. Equal 2 for the month of September.
4. Equal 2 for the month of October
5. Same methodology as 2, 3 and 4 for the months of November and December. At the bottom we find the projected total revenue compared to budgeted figures—based on the order backlog.

Projections

There are other ways of making year-end projections—like the 4 simple methods that we apply in the table below. Here we have assumed that the result as of July is the 5732 shown in the table above. Management wants to make projections in order to have an indication of what the results will be at the end of the year. We apply 4 different methods. Three of them show that it is very likely that we will not be able to reach the budgeted revenue result.

Projections of coming months' results based on 4 methods								
	Y-T-D July	Aug	Sept	Oct	Nov	Dec	Budget	Actual/ Budget
Method 1								
Year-to-date July + average for the first 7 months in the remaining months	5 732	6 551	7 370	8 189	9 007	9 826	11 750	(1 924)
% of budget	48.8 %	55.8 %	62.7 %	69.7 %	76.7 %	83.6 %	100.0 %	-16.4 %
Method 2								
Year-to-date + budget for remaining months	5 732	6 915	8 099	9 232	10 182	11 132	11 750	(618)
% of budget	48.8 %	58.9 %	68.9 %	78.6 %	86.7 %	94.7 %	100.0 %	-5.3 %
Method 3								
Year-to-date + management's assessment per month	5 732	1 460	1 220	1 300	1 200	1 150		
Projection per month		7 182	8 402	9 702	10 902	12 052	11 750	302
% of budget	48.8 %	61.1 %	71.5 %	82.6 %	92.8 %	102.6 %	100.0 %	2.6 %
Method 4								
Last year's achievement rates (%) per month	52.1 %	60.2 %	68.9 %	79.5 %	88.6 %	100.0 %		
applied on the remaining months of the year will give the following results	5 732	6 623	7 580	8 747	9 748	11 002	11 750	(748)

Conclusion 1:	If you assume that the average per month during the first seven months will repeat itself in the following five months the year-end result will be 1.924 below budget
Conclusion 2:	If we manage to achieve the budgeted result per month during the remainder of the year, the result will be 618 under budget
Conclusion 3:	Here we assume that management has made an assessment of what they will reach in each of the remaining months. The result is 302 over budget.
Conclusion 4:	Last year's achievement per month applied to the remainder of the months gives a result that is 748 under the budget for the year.

In the example above I have shown what we can do to make projections for the revenue. However, the same approaches may be applied when projecting cost and expense as well.

In such a situation with (1) Year-to-date revenues that are below plan and (2) most projections seem to confirm that we will not reach our targets, the head of the company has to initiate a process to determine the type of corrective actions that are required to bring the company back on track and help them to reach the budget. The fortunate thing is that there are several months until the year end—so in theory there is time to correct the situation.

It is most important to insure that the budgeted profit objective will be met. There are several things that the management group can initiate:

1. To boost the revenue they can initiate actions like

   o   More advertising to increase volumes
   o   Promotional offers
   o   Sales competition among the sales force—either own sales representative or dealers

   o   Various discounts that propose attractive prices to the customers—however, not so significant that they cut the revenue streams too much

2. To curb cost and expense the company could

   o   Stop or delay hiring of new staff
   o   Reduce travel
   o   Lay off staff
   o   Delay events that have been planned but are not impacting the results
   o   Increase sign-off levels for expenses beyond a certain level
   o   Negotiate better terms with suppliers

2

The Profitability Phase

Wherever we happen to be, we must treasure our manpower and material resources, and must not take a short view and indulge in wastefulness and extravagance. Wherever we are, from the very first year of our work we must bear in mind the many years to come, the protracted war that must be maintained, the counter-offensive, and the work of reconstruction after the enemy's expulsion. On the one hand, never be wasteful and extravagant; on the other actively expand production. Previously, in some places people suffered a great deal because they did not take the long view and neglected economy in manpower and expansion of production. The lesson is there and attention must be called to it.

"We Must Learn to Do Economic Work" (January 10, 1945)
Selected Works, Vol. III, p. 244 LRB 185.

We should always use our brains and think everything over carefully. A common saying goes, "Knit your brows and you will hit upon a stratagem". In other words, much thinking yields wisdom. In order to get rid of the blindness, which exists to a serious extent in our party, we must encourage our comrades to think, to learn the method of analysis and to cultivate the habit of analysis.

"Our Study and the Current Situation" (April 12, 1944)
Selected Works, Vol. III, pp. 174-75. LRB 224.

The educational policy of the college is to cultivate a firm and correct political orientation, an industrious and simple style of work, and flexible strategy and tactics. These are three essentials in the making of a . . . . revolutionary soldier. It is in accordance with these essentials that the staffs teach and students study.

To Be Attacked by the Enemy is Not a Bad Thing, But a Good Thing.
(May 26, 1939), 1st pocket ed., p. 3. LRB 146.

Don't wait until problems pile up and cause a lot of trouble before trying to solve them. Leaders must march ahead of the movement, not lag behind it.

Introductory note to "Contract on a Seasonal Basis" (1955)
The SocialistUpsurge in China's Countryside, Chinese ed., Vol. III. LRB 229.

To take such an attitude is to seek truth from facts. "Facts" are all the things that exist objectively, "truth" means their internal relations, that is, the laws governing them, and "to seek" means to study. We should proceed from the actual conditions inside and outside this country, the province, country or district, and derive from them, as to our guide to action, laws which are inherent in them and not imaginary, that is, we should find the internal relations of the events occurring around us. And in order to do that we must rely not on subjective imagination, not on momentary enthusiasm, not on lifeless books, but on facts that exist objectively; we must appropriate the material in detail and, guided by the general principles of Marxism-Leninism, draw correct conclusions from it.

"Reform our Study" (May 1941) Selected Works,
Vol. III. pp. 22-23. LRB 231.

When the control stage is over you should have a stable company with an organization that is functioning, a stable and profitable financial situation, a customer base that provides income for you every month, some quality assurance efforts and a management information system that helps you monitor the company. However, there are things that you are not happy with. You believe that there is a possibility for expansion, you and the board would like to see higher profitability, you believe that there are new markets for your existing products—maybe abroad—your organization should be able to cope with more products, you do not have sufficient control over your customers' total value chain. You have read in trade magazines and newspapers about other companies' success. In other words, despite the fact that you are doing fairly well you want to climb to higher altitudes, realize your big-time ambitions or make the dream of your life come true. In other words you are now into the Growth Phase

Let's now discuss how you can make this happen.

Strategic Plan

While you up until now have thrived with annual, relatively short-term budgets, your ambitions require you to start developing a strategic plan that has a horizon that goes beyond the next year or two and stretches 4-5 years into the future. The amazing experience that I have had—an experience that has been supported by many observations by others—is that very few management teams spend sufficient time looking into the future.

In a mind-provoking article called "Seeing the Future First" by Gary Hamel and C. K. Prahaladad in *Fortune* magazine for September 5, 1994 they contend very strongly that Senior Executives spend far too little time on external issues, f.ex. understanding the implications of new technology. Then they question how much time that is spent on looking outward, focussing on how different the world will be in 5-10 years compared to the time that is spent on worrying about the next contract or how to respond to the latest move of competition. Finally, they ask how much time is spent together with colleagues to build a shared vision of the future. Their observations result in the conclusion that senior management devotes less than 3% of its energy in building a corporate perspective of the future. In some companies the figure is less than 1%.

They contend that to develop a prescient and distinctive point of view about the future, a senior management team must be willing to spend 20% to 50% of its time over a period of months and continually revisit their points of view and adjust them as the future unfolds.

> *"The vital step in competing for the future is the quest for industry foresight. This is the race to gain an understanding deeper than competitors, of the trends and discontinuities—technological, demographic, regulatory, or lifestyle that could be used to transform industry boundaries and create new competitive space.*
>
> *Industry foresight gives a company the potential to get to the future first and stake out a leadership position. It informs corporate direction and lets a company control the evolution of its industry and, thereby, its own destiny. The trick is "to see the future before it arrives".*

The final quote from this extremely important article—which is one of the few in my collection of classics—is the following:

> *"Could you sustain a debate for a full day, among yourselves, about the implications of this trend to your company and your industry? Do you*

understand how fast this trend is emerging in different markets around the world, the technologies that are propelling it, the technology choices competitors are making, which companies are in the lead, who has the most to gain and to lose, the investment strategies of your competitors vis à vis this trend, and the variety of ways in which this trend may influence customer demands and needs?"

You and your management team must be in control of the situation and the purpose of the strategic work of your company is to gain and maintain that control.

There are many ways of making a strategic plan; one is probably no better than the other. Personally, I believe that the most important thing is to have a method and a plan for how to make such a plan. The following is the methodology that I suggest—but I repeat, there are many others. The following is inspired by my contact with Rob Eskridge of Growth Management Centre in Truckee, California.

A. Analyze the Company's Situation

The first thing we need to do is to analyze the situation of the company—what is the business environment, what are the crossroad issues that we are facing, what information do we have about the industry structure and the competitors, how has our company been developing lately, how does this development compare with the former strategic projections that have been made. In this phase we gather a lot of data, we convert it into knowledge and use it to its maximum potential in the strategic plan work.

A common way of analyzing the company situation is to make a SWOT-analysis. This acronym stands for Strengths and Weaknesses, Opportunities and Threats. The two first are a current analysis of the company's situation, while the two latter relate to the future and what would give positive rewards if we take advantage of the opportunities and what factors could create an adverse impact if we do not minimize the impact of the possible threats that we may be exposed to. A practical way of organizing this work is to fill in the following matrix:

Strengths	Weaknesses
• S	• W
• S	• W
• S	• W
• S	• W
• S	• W
• S	• W
• S	• W
Opportunities	**Threats**
• O	• T
• O	• T
• O	• T
• O	• T
• O	• T
• O	• T
• O	• T

The beginning of identifying your SWOTs could be to arrange brainstorming-sessions where various parts of your organization participate. Here you follow the rules for brainstorming. Through these brainstormings you will in addition to crossroad issues, understand the business environment, the industry structure, be identifying points related your products, your markets, your organization's skills and competence. Some items will be of internal character that you and your organization more or less are mastering and controlling, while other points will be externally oriented and as such difficult for you to control. After having got the points identified, you may want to substantiate them by gathering more information in order to face the next point.

B. Reach Conclusions about the Situation and Identify Strategic Development Areas

Based on the fact-finding that has been done above, you and your team should now be ready to reach some conclusions about the industry situation, the company situation and the competitors' situation. You are in a position to identify a number of necessary actions that you have to take to improve your market position, to strengthen your company as regards product development, to enhance your competence and skills, your quality, your productivity, your procedures and a whole host of things that you consider to be important. You can divide these actions in two—one group contains *imperatives* that urgently need to be done and the other group are *wants* that it could be nice to do—but the world is not going under if you do not attend to them for the moment. As part of the process, you should identify what we could call strategic development areas. These are areas that you and your management team should consider extremely important and have a plan for addressing. What they are depends very much on the type of business that you are in—but let me in the following try to give you some examples of such strategic development areas. Under each of these strategic development areas I think that it is important to establish strategic goals and strategic crossroads. This may of course vary from company to company but to illustrate my point, I will give you some examples of strategic goals and strategic crossroads that I have proposed to one of my clients. The strategic goals and the crossroad issues that must be taken are—of course—a function of the SWOT analysis that has resulted in conclusions made about the situation.

This was a one page summary of the most important conclusion that we arrived at after the analysis of this company:

- Lack of clarification about the choice between introduction of modern industrialization and the old production methods
- No top manager that holds things together
- Significant dependency on a few key persons
- Unclear organizational structure
- No system and principles to monitor the financial and other performance measurements
- No conscientious focus on Information and Communications Technology
- Unacceptable lead times between order and delivery
- No quality focus or quality management
- Core competencies can easily vanish
- Weak gross profit despite high prices to the customer
- Lack of ability to execute and implement decisions and plans

Based on this, the board of the company concluded that it was imperative to develop a company that was very much different from that we were seeing at the time. Behind each of these bullets there is, of course, a lot of analysis and facts to substantiate and support each of the statements.

C. Commit to a Future Direction

Together with the facts gathered in the above process we should determine where you want to go in the future

- o What line of business should we be in?
- o What are our markets?
- o What kind of policies should we have?
- o What kind of numerical development are we heading for—expressed in absolute numbers and % growth?
- o Sales volumes
- o Revenue
- o Expense growth
- o Staffing
- o Productivity
- o How should we be organized?

D. Strategic Development Areas

As a result of this, a number of strategic development areas were identified and developed. These were:

- **Organization and Management**

  - **Strategic Goal**—To develop the organization so that it is capable of handling the challenges that they will be facing today and in the future like management, innovation, market orientation, planning and control, design and product development, Information and Communications Technology
  - **Strategic Crossroad Issues**—to select a management group that can hold the company together and bring it forward.

- **Design and Product Development**

  - **Strategic Goals**—organize the design and product development efforts so that we foster creativity and ascertain an influx of ideas from many sources—internally and externally—in a systematic way; survey the market and the trends systematically; understand customer needs; insure that we inspire our own staff and other parties that are involved so that we attract customers; develop and retain competence. We shall emphasize quality, functionality and design and take the customer focus away from price.
  - **Strategic Crossroad Issues**—should we be producing innovative products or following trends; what is the life cycle of our products, what additional functionality and value shall we give the customers, who are the external resources that we should engage in this process and how should we organize this effort.

This subject is more thoroughly handled in a later chapter.

- **Market and Distribution**

  - **Strategic Goals**—Establish one sales and marketing organization that can develop and extend today's distribution channels, establish new channels, develop the markets for our product portfolio, operate the sales and marketing effort in a professional and customer-oriented way, increase the customer value and develop new income streams, establish strategic alliances and partnerships.
  - **Strategic Crossroad Issues**—Move from today's fragmented sales and marketing effort to one forceful unit under one management, decide where the sales force should be located, develop communications and brand building programs, decide if we should go into the export market.

- **Production**—remember my previous definition of production

  - **Strategic Goals**—Improve the gross margin to 55-60%, reduce the lead times through more efficient processes from the time the order is taken until the delivery has been made, 20-40% productivity improvements through better utilization of the production capacity, profit-oriented management of time and material, planning of delivery time and improvement in the skills of the operators.

- **Strategic Crossroad Issues**—Move to industrialized production and away from the handicraft-oriented processes that we have had up until now using more outsourcing and ties to strategic partners, organize production so that it is less dependent on manual labor through using sub-suppliers, assembly of semi raw material, standardization and fewer models, minimize taylor-making, quality control, efficient logistics and efficient production systems.

- **Logistics**

  - **Strategic Goals**—Efficient logistics must be part of our core competencies and contribute solidly to profitability improvements, reduction of lead times, improved quality and improved customer satisfaction, optimization of the physical inventories to reduce capital binding and inventory costs, avoid obsolescence, minimize risk of not being able to deliver. Transport in and out to be done by external transporters.
  - **Strategic Crossroad Issues**—Inventory management systems, number of variations, choice of strategic partners particularly in the transportation area.

- **Strategic Partnerships**

  - **Strategic Goals**—Define the areas in which we want to use strategic partners; develop a "Strategic Partner Policy" to describe how we want to use them and what we shall demand from them.
  - **Strategic Crossroad Issues**—Review of the existing portfolio of strategic partners and decide who shall be with us in the future; find new strategic partners in light of the new strategic orientation of the company.

CHAIRMAN MAO'S BUSINESS SCHOOL

- **Information and Communications Technology (ICT)**

  - **Strategic Goals**—Make ICT a kingpin in the corporate development that shall contribute to increased productivity, improved profitability and better control, make the investments necessary to make ICT a tool that dramatically will improve our ability to master the changes that we are facing in the future, improve the staffs' ability to take advantage of the possibilities that ICT offers.
  - **Strategic Crossroad Issues**—Decide on the future system platform; decide on how to organize the ICT-function—do it ourselves or outsource it. Establish a (generous) budget to acquire the hardware and software that is required.

- **Management Control Systems**

  - **Strategic Goals**—We must establish management control systems that insure that our direction is right i.e. towards our mission, vision, objectives, budgets and action plans (financial and non-financial), strategies and critical success factors. The systems must inform us about increase in values, about the company's ability to implement its overall objectives and put the management in a position to improve the company's performance.
  - **Strategic Crossroad Issues**—Decide on who our customers are and what we shall deliver to them (our mission)? What is our desired picture of the future (vision)? What shall we achieve in the different areas (overall goals)? Strategic choices (what choices do we have to realize our mission, vision and overall goals; what is required to reach the overall goals and strategies, what must be in place and what must not go wrong)? What indicators must we focus on in order to steer in the right direction and what are the required levels (monitoring parameters)? What concrete actions must be taken, who is responsible, what are the milestones, when are we going to reach them, how and when shall we report? (action plans).

- **Total Quality Management**

  - **Strategic Goals**—Quality is a top-management responsibility and everybody should be obsessed by the idea of delivering quality of high value in all relations that we have with "our customers". Therefore, goals—particularly quantitative—need to be established to monitor what we want to achieve in the quality area. Our attainment of these goals must be measured continuously in order to ascertain that we are delivering or are moving towards the quality that we are aiming at. When we do not reach our goals we should understand why and eradicate the reasons for not reaching them. Our efforts in this area shall be documented through an ISO-process. We should also understand what does bad quality cost us.

  - **Strategic Crossroad Issues**—Who is responsible for the quality effort in addition to the fact that this is a top-management responsibility, how do we create quality consciousness among the employees, suppliers, dealers and others whose behavior impacts society's perception of us as a quality organization and what should be the quality measurements that we establish in areas like procurement, product development, production, order processing, planning and control, administration and control, information and communication.

- **Industry Structure**

  - **Strategic Goals**—We want to be proactive—i.e to play a lead role and influence the development—in the effort to modernize our industry and to become a strong operator in this segment of our industry. Furthermore, we want this new unit to change the perception of what our products and services can be for our customers and that our name will be a "household word" among the potential consumers of our products and services.

  - **Strategic Crossroad Issues**—Decide what the most important criteria for selecting merger partners are and identify potential partners that should be evaluated.

Market Development

What Did Mao Say?

Even if we achieve gigantic successes in our work, there is no reason whatsoever to feel conceited and arrogant. Modesty helps one to get forwards, whereas conceit makes one lag behind. This is a truth that we must always bear in mind.

"Opening Address at the Eighth National Congress of the Communist Party of China" (September 11, 1956). LRB 237.

Our Army has always two policies. First, we must be ruthless to our enemies, we must overpower and annihilate them. Second, we must be kind to our own, to the people, to our comrades and to our superiors and subordinates, and unite with them.

Speech at the Reception given by the Central Committee of the Party for Model Study Delegates from the Rear Army Detachment (September 18, 1944). LRB 148.

The educational policy of the college is to cultivate a firm and correct political orientation, an industrious and simple style of work, and flexible strategy and tactics. These are three essentials in the making of a . . . . revolutionary soldier. It is in accordance with these essentials that the staff teaches and students study.

To Be Attacked by the Enemy is Not a Bad Thing, But a Good Thing. (May 26, 1939) 1st pocket ed. p. 3. LRB 146.

In all the practical work of our party, all correct leadership is necessarily "from the masses, to the masses". This means: take the ideas of the masses (scattered and unsystematic ideas) and concentrate them (through study turn them into systematic and systematic ideas), then go to the masses and propagate and explain these ideas until the masses embrace them as their own, hold fast to them and translate them into action, and test the correctness of these ideas into such action. Then once again concentrate ideas from the masses and once again go to the masses so that the ideas are persevered in and carried through. And so on, over and over again in an endless spiral, with the ideas becoming more correct, more vital and richer each time. Such is the Marxist theory of knowledge.

"Some Questions Concerning Methods of Leadership" (June 1, 1943), Selected Works, Vol. III, p. 119. LRB 128.

To link oneself with the masses one must act in accordance with the needs and wishes of the masses. All work done for the masses must start from their needs and not from the desire of any individual, however well-intentioned. It often happens that objectively the masses need a certain change, but subjectively, they are not yet conscious of the need, not yet willing or determined to make the change. In such cases we should wait patiently. We should not make the change until, through our work, most of the masses become conscious of the need and are willing and determined to carry it out. Otherwise we shall isolate ourselves from the masses. Unless they are conscious and willing, any kind of work that requires their participation will turn out to be more formality and will fail. . . . There are two principles here: One is the actual needs of the masses rather than what we fancy they need, and the other is the wishes of the masses, who must take up their own minds instead of our making their minds for them.

"The United Front in Cultural Work" (October 30, 1944)
Selected Works, Vol. III, pp. 236-37. LRB 124.

Among the most important issues that you will have to address in strategic work is what products and services you are offering and what markets and customers are expected to have a demand for these products and services. In the beginning of a company's life, the focus is on a limited market, a limited customer set, a limited application for your products and services. The reason for this is lack of knowledge, lack of financial resources, lack of competence etc. However, as time passes, you gain information and build up financial resources that make it possible for you to have a wider outlook, new ideas and a bolder attitude. If you have been successful, the old saying that "Success breeds success" applies, and you might be ready for climbing to new heights. However, to do this you need a practical approach—an approach that helps you to identify new markets and new customers for your existing product portfolio and new products and services for your existing products and services. To execute this systematic approach I have found that the diagram on the next page is very useful. The diagram should be self-explanatory—and I recommend that you gather your people for a brainstorming where you apply the brainstorming methods that have been described above.

You may start by filling in the lower left-hand quadrant by describing what your products and services are today. This is in itself an interesting exercise. When I meet a management group for the first time, I often ask them what they offer to their markets and their customers. I am often extremely surprised to learn how imprecise they are in describing what they are selling. All companies should have a detailed description of their products and services. They should also ask what they are charging for and what they are not charging for. Through this latter exercise you may often find out that you are giving the customers a lot of freebees that you should try to get them to pay for rather than giving them away for free.

In the helicopter industry, the customers were in fact charged on a per minute basis although the prices were quoted per hour. With tens and thousands of stops and starts during the year—a minute earlier start and minute later stops amounted to large amounts of money every year. This was in fact in accordance with the service agreement. However, the pilots wanted to be nice to their customers and therefore they had their own interpretation of what a start and a stop was. The same applied to auxiliary equipment—ropes, big-bags, nets, cameras and other things that we used to execute the mission. To charge for such things would have been fully accepted.

Where to Find Market Opportunities

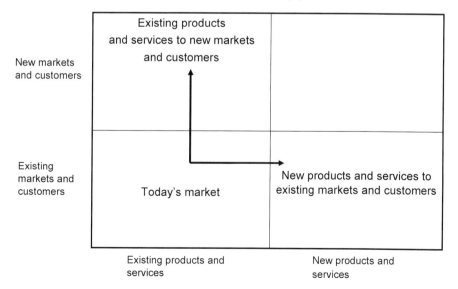

Very often your sales representatives—particularly in service industries—give away freebees by classifying things as marketing expense, while in fact it clearly is a billable product or service. In other words, examine your business practices and see whether it is reasonable to charge for things that you currently are giving away for free. The interesting thing is that normally there is no cost of products or services associated with these extras and the revenue yield flows directly down to the "bottom line". The same often applies to your discount practice. You should also study this thoroughly.

Let's examine some of the things that you could do in the lower right hand quadrant where we examine **new** products and services to **existing** markets and customers. There might be a number of opportunities for revenue additions in analyzing the opportunities that you have.

- First of all, you could strengthen your revenue base by classifying some of the things that you up until now have given away for free—ref. the above comments—and classify them as product and service additions and offer them to your existing customers.

- The next step is to identify associated products and services that you could develop into marketable products and services. There are numerous examples of this. One example could be the aftermarket for a car dealer or a car manufacturer. There are virtually no limits to the products and services that they may develop for enthusiastic car owners with purchasing power. An owner of cinemas might establish a little café or kiosk to sell snacks, drinks, chocolate, film-magazines etc. to the customers that are coming to watch his shows.

- Another way to improve you earnings from existing customers and markets is to get a larger part of the "total value chain". Let's say that you are a furniture manufacturer that sells your products to furniture stores around the country. The value chain of the furniture business is raw materials, semi-manufactured components, fabrics, manufacturing of the finished goods, transportation, logistics, retailing, financing, repair, the second-hand market, disposal when the product is worn out. If you are only assembling the furniture using raw materials, you might study the possibilities of taking over the manufacturing of the semi-raw material components. You might also evaluate the possibilities of opening retail stores to sell directly to the customers. Maybe you want to help the customers finance their purchases. A partnership with a financing institution might give you access to an interesting revenue stream. When I was a young manager in IBM I remember the profitable revenue streams that were generated when we established a leasing business for EDP (IT)—equipment.

- A fourth dimension is to see if any of the core competencies that we have can be used to create new revenue streams. One extremely telling example of this is Gillette, the global producer of shaving and beauty products. A couple of years ago they bought Duracell, the battery manufacturer. A major reason for this—I believe—was that Duracell reached their customers to a large extent through the same distribution channels as Gillette's shaving and beauty products. Thus they could take advantage of each other's customer bases, logistical systems, billing systems etc.
- One company that I advised on strategic matters had a very efficient logistics system and we asked ourselves what kind of other products could you distribute to your existing customers utilizing this core competency. As a consequence, other products in addition to the traditional products filled the trucks every night.

Existing products and services to new markets and customers

Ask yourselves where we can find new customers to our existing products. Use the same brainstorming approach that I have recommended above. Gather your best people to solve this problem—you may even supplement the group with outside consultants. Ask them where we can sell our existing products and technology to new customers.

- Ask the group if there are any new geographical areas where you could develop a profitable distribution. This could either be in a different region of the country or you may even be thinking about export to other countries.
- Are there any new customer groups that could take advantage of the technology that you use in your main product? One example of this

is the Sony Walkman. What Sony did was minimize the technology used in the hi-fi sets that they sold to homes to make it possible to be carried around by teenagers and other people on the move. According to the story, this idea came from Akio Morita, the founder of Sony in the early 1980's. He got a lot of resistance from his younger well-educated engineers and marketing experts. They did not have any confidence in the "old man's" idea. However, as he was the boss, they had to succumb to his wishes. And you all know what a tremendous success the Walkman became for Sony. It is also interesting to note that Walkman, which was a product name, ended up by being the generic name for a product with the features of this mobile unit. There are numerous examples of applying a proven technology to different areas.

- Look at the customers of your competitors. You, of course, want to have most of them as your customers. However, in order to be practical, single out those that you most want in your own base, make a plan for how to make them your customers and approach them. One way of starting is to meet with them to understand what problems they are facing today and how you might be able to help them.

Existing and New Products to Existing and New Markets and New Customers

This is the result that you end up with in the upper right-hand quadrant and is really the sum of the three other quadrants. I believe that this is a very simple approach, but as I have said before, a simple analysis and approach is certainly better than nothing. It is a start that you could refine as you move deeper into your own process.

Use your imagination and your competent colleagues to identify possibilities that fit into the three new quadrants. Analyze and investigate the opportunities, draw your conclusions and make decisions on this basis. Keep in mind that the more relationships that you have and the deeper the relationships with a customer are, the more attached to you he becomes and the more difficult it is to break out of the relationship.

How to raise capital to finance the company development

In most cases you will need to raise capital to finance the development of your company. There are many ways of doing this and I refer to the section about Cash Flow and Liquidity earlier in the book. To supplement my thoughts there I would like to refer to the 6 points below written by Lyve Alexis Pleshette who is a staff writer of Power Homebiz Guides—http://www. powerhomebiz.com. The six points convey very well the things that you should have in mind whether you business is starting up or is a more mature company that needs funding for charging further ahead.

"1. Finding Investors

Without a doubt, finding potential investors for your business is the hardest part of raising capital. You may start within your family circles, your friends, your business associates and acquaintances. Then you can approach institutional sources of funds, such as banks and even the government. Once you find the right person or institution willing to finance your business, your business plan will do most of the talking. The first step should occupy about half of the entire time used to prepare and present a business plan. Most entrepreneurs fail to do this step well and, consequently, fail at raising capital.

2. The Approach

During the approach, two things must occur. First, you should seek to reduce tension in your relationship with the venture source. While it may at times seem like an adversarial relationship, it is important to remember your goal is to make money together. Second, the entrepreneur should simultaneously be building a degree of task tension. As relationship tension is reduced, a reciprocal concern about building up the task at hand should occur. The venture source needs to invest capital, and you need to raise capital. Fulfilling your mutual needs is the task you must accomplish together.

3. Qualifying the Source

After identifying potential sources of funds, the next step is to ask, "Why will they be interested in funding my business?" Every possible funding source has a "hot button" that you need to push for that person to agree with the deal. Not everyone invests in the same deals for the same reasons, as certain benefits among the features will be more important to individual capital sources than others. In fact, the same plan is likely to be supported by different people for different reasons. You need to identify the needs and reasons for investing of your potential money source. Study the fund source's portfolio and needs.

4. Presenting the Business Plan

The presentation of the business plan is an area that entrepreneurs can be expected to do well. They are so familiar with their product, having lived with it night and day, that they can always make a convincing presentation. However, the benefit to the potential investors is an element that should be sufficiently highlighted. Don't dazzle investors with your knowledge of the latest technology or understanding of the market—stick to explaining the benefits of your business concept.

What is the perceived value of your product vs. what your product actually does? What are its features? Why will everyone need your product or service? What will it replace? What is it most similar to? What will happen to your customers if they don't buy your product or service?

5. Handling Objections

As an entrepreneur, you should always expect objection to your business plan—from the product concept, to your approach, to your marketing strategies, or any apparent weakness of your plan or your product. Some will also ask you, "What are you going to do that's different, and how are you going to do it better than what is already being done?" In handling objections, the first thing to avoid is to be defensive. Instead, acknowledge the comment, and respond to the objection in a sincere way.

Empathize with it, legitimize it, and then introduce new information to counter the objection. Occasionally, objections stem because they are only partially informed, but they are never wrong. Your job is to have all the facts on hand so you can turn the objection around—turn a no into a yes.

6. Gaining the Commitment

If the first five steps are handled carefully, then gaining the commitment will be the easiest and least stressful step in the entire process. To gain a commitment, you need to close any objections your potential investors may have had and turn it around in your favor. Remember, your enthusiasm and "entrepreneurial fire" are two elements that most investors will look for."

Handling the Profitability Phase right with particular emphasis on the development of a strategic plan, continuos market development and ensuring that you have a liquidity situation that gives you freedom to handle, you get access to new markets and new customers with new products. The sum of this is new revenue streams which also might come from getting more of your customers' value chain.

3

The Growth Phase

Having taken your company through the Control and Profitability phases, you should assume that the necessary controls are in place and the financial situation is strong enough to sustain risks. In other words, you are into the growth phase. Growth—normally—comes from four areas:

- Organic growth
- Partnering
- Mergers and aquisitions
- Establishment in new geographies

All need financial strength and attention from the management and before you make moves in these areas you must ascertain that there is sufficient management capacity to look after whatever moves you intend to make. It is not uncommon to expand without having this in mind.

I am writing this in-flight back to my hometown after having attended a board meeting, where I am chairman. The subject was where are we going? Three alternatives were on the table.

- Expansion through establishing a branch abroad
- An internal consolidation that would make it possible to enhance IT-services revenue through consolidation of the company's resources in this area.
- Acquisition of a company in the same industry with presence in other cities than where we are located now—cities where we wanted to establish presence.

Our very energetic general manager wanted to do all three things. To this the board put its foot down. Notwithstanding all his energy and positive intentions, the board said that we had to focus and prioritize. It is easy to take on a lot of new tasks particularly if they are exciting and challenging as well as adventurous as my good general manager said. However, it is important to give attention to the current business and always remember that there will be some things that will not develop as desired. This was a point that the board stressed. Consequently, we had to make a choice of one or maximum two of the alternatives and let the one or two that we abandoned remain abandoned. In order to make a rationale decision, we established a few criteria that were important. In this case they were:

❖ **Reasonable Risk** with dimensions like

- Size of investment
- Start of revenue streams
- Payback time
- Return on investments
- Market knowledge
- Competition
- Required management attention and focus
- Likelihood of success

❖ **Maximize Stockholder Value** within a reasonable period of time.

- Payback time
- Return on investment
- Dilution of earnings

Based on these two sets of criteria, we decided to abandon establishment abroad and to pursue the two other alternatives.

Prioritization is an important part of management's job. Interesting opportunities come across the desk all the time. It might be tempting to see all the upsides and easily forget that rainy days will come in connection with most of the things you enter into. These rainy days may take attention away from the other tasks that you have. Therefore assess all the aspects of the new situation, establish criteria for decision-making, make the decisions and stick with it. I have all too often experienced that decisions that are made in one meeting are re-opened in the next. Let's look at some ways of expanding the business:

Organic Growth

The organic growth in revenue and profit is coming from enhancement of the current business, i.e. increase in the revenue of existing activities. This can be done by selling more of your existing products either by more sales to existing customers or to new customers. You may realize growth by adding some new products to your current product portfolio or take some out that no longer show the sales potential they used to have and replace them with similar products with more functions, higher quality, or such to improve the revenue per unit.

This may also be achieved by increasing your production capacity to turn out more products. Here you have the following options: (1) To increase the production capacity you may have to hire more people or buy new faster machinery, (2) you may increase the productivity of your machines by tuning their speed and your people by inducing them to work faster or (3) you might also turn out more products by working two or three shifts and train your pepople to work smarter and more efficiently. However, there are limits to the growth that you can achieve through the organic measures that may be available.

Partnering

Another way of increasing your business might be different alternatives for partnering. Through this you might sign agreements with your partners that will give you new business because the partners refer business to you. Let me give you a few examples.

In the airline industry it is nowadays common to be part of a large network that in total consists of several airlines so that it is possible to provide an easy and comfortable journey to any place in the world. One example of this is Star Alliance that consists of airlines from all over the world. I found the following in Wikipedia that describes the purpose of the alliance: *"The **Star Alliance**,* *launched on May 14, 1997, is the largest and most awarded airline alliance in the world, with the following points of cooperation among its partner airlines:*

- *Frequent flyer program integration allows airline miles to be earned and redeemed on all members of the Alliance at the same level*
- *Premium customers of the alliance have access to all members' airport lounges.*
- *Flight schedules are coordinated to permit almost seamless travel which may include several different carriers within the alliance, on a single ticket*
- *Special fares for round-the-world and similar travel on alliance members offer discounts over booking individual itineraries*
- *Customer service processes are harmonized in an effort to promote a consistent experience*
- *Cooperation in development of a common information technology platform"*

Members of the alliance are Albania Airline, Austrian (Austria), British Midland (UK), LOT (Poland), Lufthansa (Germany), Scandianavian Airlines (Denmark, Norway and Sweden), Singapore Airlines, South African, Spanair (Spain), Swiss (Switzerland), TAP (Portugal), Thai (Thailand), United Airlines (US), US Airways (US), Varig (Brasil) pluss a number of affiliated regional airlines. The alliance now runs 16.930 daily flights to 842 airports in 152 cities. Its market share in 2005 was 28%. With this list of impressive competitive national carriers it is no wonder why the alliance offers *"almost seamless travel which may include several different carriers within the alliance, on a single ticket."* The creation of the Star Alliance was a milestone in airline history due to its size and sparked the formation of rivals, notably *Oneworld* and *SkyTeam*.

There are many, many other examples of such types of co-operation in many industries all over the world. Another example could be the hotel industry. A live proof of this is just to pick up one of the leading hotel chains' rooster of participating hotels next time you stay at such a hotel.

One must, however, observe the competition rules and laws when such partnerships are constructed so that such tight cooperation does not lead to suspicion of anti-competitive behavior. Very often such partnerships are operated within the framework of a franchise system, where there are individual owners, whose companies are sewn together by common branding, operational manuals, commonality as far as products are concerned and many other factors. The participants pay normally a fee—often called royalty—that is providing means to develop things that should be common for the partners and to provide a profit to the franchisor. Sometimes there is also a one-off franchise fee to be a member of such a network.

Mergers, acquisitions and other partnerships

The big time growth in revenue is normally attained through mergers with or acquisitions of other companies. However, the sad fact is that this growth does not necessarily result in a comparable increase in the profit of the two companies or result in other intended benefits of the partnership. Let's start off with a list of reasons why companies believe that they should merge with another company:

- Increased sales
- Improved competitiveness
- Development of new products and services
- Improved logistics capacity
- Efficient product development and improved innovative capability
- Financial resources
- Reduced risk

Whether we talk about a merger or an acquisition, it is a question of partnering with somebody that you do not know at all or only have a faint knowledge about in the first place. It is therefore extremely important to make sure that conditions exist that make the relationship successful. At the same time, we should note that a large number of the partnerships that are being entered into end up not being what one hoped for at the time of the agreement. Let me illustrate this sad fact:

- A former GE top strategic planner said : *"Nine out of ten acquisitions are a waste of time and a destruction of shareholder value".*

- In a study made by McKinsey over a ten year period that comprised 200 of the largest public corporations, they determined that a mere 23% were successful (as measured by an increase in stockholder value). They found that the most successful acquisitions (33%) were found with small acquisitions in related areas while the lowest success resulted from mergers of large firms whose operations were in unrelated areas.
- An economist at the Securities and Exchange Commission was quoted as follows: *"You don't put two turkeys together and make an eagle".*
- Pierre Halbron, Managing Director of Wasserstein Perella in France, said that: *"Acquisition is unsuccessful in most cases because there is an incompatibility of cultures".*

I can support this by my own experience and observations. In many cases management attention and focus were lacking because of the egos of the CEO's that were impacted by the merger plans. Two significant cases come to my mind: One was a proposed merger of two of the world's largest pharmaceutical companies that failed because the two egocentric CEOs could not agree as to who should be at the helm after the merger. Consequently, a transaction that could have increased stockholder value considerably went down the drain because the two gentlemen's egos could not stand the thought that the other guy should lead the company.

A similar situation surfaced when two governments tried to merge two national monopolies. The top men could not agree about the top positions and the negotiations were called off. In a world with a significant need for larger units in an industry calling for market power, financial strengths, and technological ability, it was crazy not to let the merger happen.

In my book, childish and selfish behavior abandoned rational transactions in these two cases. The boards or the stockholders of the two companies should have determined who the best person in a merged situation was and let the other go without losing face. Once in a while there are attempts to solve such conflicts by letting one of them become the chairman and the other the CEO. This might not be a bad idea and can represent the best of two worlds if the two persons are able to co-operate. Otherwise it is stupid and the solution is to let one of them go. I have also seen cases were it was decided that one of the contenders should have the top job for, let's say, the first two years and thereafter the other should be in charge. This is in most cases an equally bad idea.

In other words, alliances must be well constructed and the implementation tightly monitored in order to secure the expected goals and benefits. It is therefore necessary with a process that ascertains that the likelihood of a successful relationship is highly possible. There are many ways this could happen. I would like to show you what the Oslo-based Performance Group established as a viable process to secure stockholder's value as a result of a merger or partnership. This is inspired by their book *Partnering for Value*. They proposed the following phases:

o **Preparation phase**

- Identifying partnering need
- Partner selection process

o **Creation and visioning phase**

- Creating a joint vision and overall objectives for the partnership
- Setting the partnership management structure

o **Implementation and operational phase**

- Implementation of the daily management of the partnership

o **Redefining phase**

- Redefining or dissolving the partnership.

Since it may be extremely difficult to get out of a partnership that is not functioning, it is important in advance and before any commitments are made to ascertain that there are conditions on either side that support the idea.

Geographical expansion

In this globalised world, a very obvious way to grow is to establish operations in other countries or in other regions of a large country. Such an expansion can happen by creating a new company and building it from scratch. Another way of doing this is to acquire a company in the same industry with management, industry competence and a customer base. It is very important to be aware of the fact that when you start operating in a new country you will encounter an entirely different culture, different languages, different customer behaviour, different laws. The difficulties with foreign expansion—including the time it takes—should therefore not be underestimated.

The chart below summarizes the opportunities that a corporations has to grow.

Growth opportunities

Geographical expansion

Mergers & Acquistions

New business models

Organic growth with todays business models

Now

Next Year

Next Year + 1

How to find the right value of a company?

When you want to acquire or sell a company, the pricing is of course one of the main considerations in the negotiations. The basis for determining the price is the values that are booked in the accounting records. However, they often do not reflect the real values because they are often a result of year long application of accounting rules, they represent the past while when you are buying a company, you do it with the future in mind—a future that should be as bright as possible. Therefore, you have to find other factors that impact the price. The difference between the price and the booked values—basically from the Balance Sheet—is called goodwill. Recognizing this, the actual sales price may be far from the values reflected in the accounting records. In the following table you will find a number of items that impact the goodwill in a sales or acquisition situation.

Factors that impact the sales price of a corporation beyond values in the Balance Sheet (goodwill)

Description	How to use/How to compute (algorithm)
vPrice/Earnings Ratio	X*profit after (before) tax – (profit equals NBT, NAT, EBIDTA or EBIT)
vPrice/Sales Ratio	X*annual sales
vValue of the Resources	Number of professional resources* future earnings – applied in technology companies where brainware is a major asset
vCash Flow	Present value of future cash flow
vFuture Opportunities	Future opportunities in the existing and new markets for the company's products and services
vStrategic Plans	How concrete are they and how realizable are they?
vThe Management	What is the caliber of the top manager and his management team – are they willing to stay on to preserve continuity?
vBrand Name	What does it cost to build a brand – what is its future earnings opportunities?
vCustomer Base	Net present value of the future earnings of the current customer base
vPartners	Who are the strategic partners and what is their future contribution?
vSynergies	What is the value of merging the operations of the buyers and the sellers?
vIntellectual Property Rights	The anticipated value of patents, trademarks etc.

As stated above by Pierre Halbron, incompatibility of cultures is a very common reason that mergers and acquisitions are not successful. It is quite reasonable that two organizations that plan to merge or start other ways of cooperation have distinctly different cultures. This should, however, not be the reason for not carrying out plans to merge two organizations. What management should realize is that it is obvious that when you bring two different cultures together there will be a lot of incompatibility. Then they should question what is required to build a bridge between the two cultures rather than let them continue to live their separate lives. What management should do is to make a systematic analysis of the two cultures to determine what the incompatibilities are and then figure out how to bring them together in a planned and systematic fashion. In this way they can get the best out of two worlds instead of letting two worlds fight each other, believing that the prevailing attitude becomes "our way of doing things is the best". The latter is unfortunately very often the case and as a result there are two camps in the company for a number of years and instead of creating synergies, you create devastating conflicts that spoil the initial intentions of the mergers.

The General Manager's role and focus during the Growth Phase

What Did Mao Say?

We must never adopt an arrogant attitude of great-power chauvinism and become conceited because of the victory of our revolution and certain achievements in our construction. Every nation—big or small—has its weak points.

"Opening Address at the Eighth National Congress of the Communist Party of China" (September 15, 1956). LRB 180.

You have many good qualities and have rendered great service, but you must always remember not to become conceited. You are respected by all, and quite rightly, but this easily leads to conceit. If you become conceited, if you are not modest and cease to exert yourselves, and if you do not respect others, do not respect the cadres and the masses, then you will cease to be heroes and models. There have been such people in the past, and I hope you will not follow their example.

"We Must Learn to Do Economic Work" (January 10, 1945), Selected Works, Vol. III, p. 321. LRB 183.

Be resolute, fear no sacrifice and surmount every difficulty to win victory.

"The Foolish Old Man Who Removed the Mountains" (June 11, 1941) Selected Works, Vol. III, p. 321 LBR 182.

A dangerous tendency has shown itself of late among many of our personnel—an unwillingness to share the joys and hardships of the masses, a concern for personal fame and gain. This is very bad. One way of overcoming it is to simplify our organisation in the course of our campaign to increase production and practise economy, and to transfer cadres to lower levels so that a considerable number will return to productive work.

On the Correct Handling of Contradictions Among the People" (February 27, 1957) 1st pocket ed., p. 71. LRB 190.

We must know how to use cadres well. In the final analysis, leadership involves two main responsibilities: to work out ideas and to use cadres well. Such things as drawing up plans, making decisions, and giving orders and directives, are all in the category of "working out ideas". To put the ideas into practice, we must weld the cadres together and encourage them to go into action; this comes into the category of "using the cadres well".

"The Role of the Chinese Communist Party in the National War" (October 1938) Selected Works, Vol. II, p. 202 LRB 282.

Our educational policy must enable everyone who receives an education to develop morally, intellectually and physically and become a worker with both socialist consciousness and culture.

On the Correct Handling of Contradictions Among the People (February 27, 1957), 1st pocket ed., p. 44. LRB 165.

As for the methods of training, we should unfold the mass training movement in which officers teach officers, soldiers teach officers and the soldiers teach each other.

"Policy for Work in the Liberated Areas for 1946" (December 15, 1945), Selected Works, Vol. IV, p. 76. LRB 168.

We must affirm anew the discipline of the Party.

1. *The individual is subordinate to the organisation;*
2. *The minority is subordinate to the majority;*
3. *The lower level is subordinate to the higher level and*
4. *The entire membership is subordinate to the Central Committee*

"The Role of the Chinese Communist Party in the National War" (October 1938) Selected Works, Vol. II, pp 203-204. LRB 255.

The Three Main Rules of Discipline are as follows:

1. *Obey orders in all your actions*
2. *Do not take a single needle or piece of thread from the masses*
3. *Turn in everything captured*

The Eight points for attention are as follows

1. *Speak politely*
2. *Pay fairly for what you buy*
3. *Return—everything you borrow*
4. *Pay for anything you damage*
5. *Do not hit or swear at people*
6. *Do not damage crops*
7. *Do not take liberties with women*
8. *Do not ill-treat captives*

"On the Reissue of the Three Main Rules of Discipline and the Eight Points for Attention—instructions of the General Headquarters of the Chinese Peoples Liberation Army" (October 10. 1947), Selected Military Writings. 2nd ed., p. 343. LRB 256.

When you have arrived at the third of the three development phases, you should have some expectations about the situation that you will be in as the head of a well-run organization.

You should be in a position where it possible for you to focus on the long-range aspects of the business. You should be able to sit down with your team and spend time evaluating the future of your company and the trends and paradigm shifts that are taking place in your industry and in the economy—nationally as well as globally. You should think long-range, big-time and strategically.

You are hopefully not too close to the daily operations so that the above becomes impossible. There are two important reasons for this: either because it is required since you do not have a management team that is capable of solving the day-to-day problems and operations of your business, or because you and your management team are not trained to enter into such a process.

You should assess whether you spend enough time doing strategic work. If not, you should try to find the reasons for this and make the changes required to involve yourself more in the strategic work of the company.

If you have a management team that constantly requires your attention to solve simple and easy operational problems, you have to force them to stand on their own feet and make the decisions that they deem right in the given situations. If this does not suffice, I suggest that you make a few changes by replacing the individuals with more capable persons, reorganize or initiate a change in your own style. Are you certain that your style is conducive to independence, risk-taking, and ability among your closest staff to do their jobs on their own? Maybe you are too control-oriented and do not accept that people have other opinions than yourself or people are afraid of your reaction when mistakes are made.

If you are not able to do the strategic planning yourself, it might be well-spent money to hire a consulting firm to help you start the process together with your closest aides and other key persons in your company. Your thinking should be visionary, big-time, long-range, creative, bordercrossing, bold and unexpected, providing enthusiasm and motivation. This will earn you and your company respect among the employees and in the eyes of the public.

You should be active in the trade organizations of the industry that you are in. If there are conditions that you want to bring to the public's attention, you should engage yourself in lobbying activities, making speeches, appearances on TV, writing articles or being interviewed by the newspapers. You should also identify the important opinion leaders—local or national—and initiate relations with them. Present your industry and your company to them and those arguments that you have for the stance that you are taking or the things that you want to achieve.

"Management by walking and travelling around" is a sentence that I've paraphrased slightly. It became well known through Thomas J. Peters and Robert H. Waterman, Jr.'s book *In Search of Exellence*. In searching for factors that were important in successful organizations the authors of the book stressed that walking around among the employees, trying to understand their viewpoints, their desires and aspirations, respond to their inquiries, understand who they are and what their interests in private life are, present the companies goals and strategies etc. were important in creating a positive, motivated and productive work force. To me it sounds to a large extent like what Chairman Mao stated about taking care of cadres.

I also believe that you need to show passion or obsession and take advantage of all opportunities to convey this to your employees. You must demonstrate that you believe in the company and its values, mission, vision, goals and strategies. You need to have some clear objectives that you repeatedly present with enthusiasm to your people. You should be obsessed with customer care and customer attention and as often as possible meet your customers. You must be a quality champion and over and over again repeat that this is something that you will not compromise on. In some cultures it also helps if you have a sense of humor.

Be a good listener. Whenever you are out in the organization meet your people, show them respect and listen to them irrespective of what level in the organization they belong to. It is particularly important to listen to the people who are close to the customers. They know where "the shoe pinches". They can therefore tell you a lot about the customers' perception of quality, product properties, our service delivery and many, many other things that are necessary to know in order to be a winner in today's fiercely competitive world.

Management training

Training is a very important discipline of your company that should be organized so that you have a work force that has all the skills required to be the best in your industry. One of your functional managers should have this as an important responsibility.

You should personally be responsible for establishing management training courses that train your young managers as well as your managers at higher levels. Remember what Mao said about taking good care of cadres: . . . . *raise their level. This means educating them by giving them the opportunity to study so that they can enhance their theoretical understanding and their working ability.*

There is a lot of work implied in this sentence and you should familiarize yourself with the training efforts of large corporations. Their reason for emphasizing this is that it makes business sense. IBM—where I worked for 17 years—considered training an extremely important issue. Consequently, they had local training centers, national training centers, regional training centers as well as global training centers. Here people met for classes of two to three days duration or up to several months. Most of the classes were international and cross-functional so that people also became acquainted with fields that were completely different from their own. This crossbreeding developed multitalented managers with many skills that could operate in different environments. The latter was important because IBM transferred people within countries as well as internationally. Having been exposed to various cultures, nationalities etc. prior to a move to a new location made the adaptation to new conditions easier. Of course, it has a value in itself to learn to respect people that come from different parts of the country and from different countries and cultures. By the way—jokingly we said that IBM was an acronym for I've Been Moved. In Tom Peters book *Thriving on Chaos*, I see that Peter Drucker said about Tom Watson, the founder of IBM: "Above all, Watson trained, and trained and trained"

When I was a general manager I emphasized that the curriculum should consist of (1) Business awareness subjects—like company mission and vision, finances, product knowledge, company policies etc. Furthermore, there should be (2) Technical training where employees are trained in salesmanship, technical service, operations, research and development, finance and accounting, managerial skills etc. In other words, knowledge that to a large extent can be applied to the students' job immediately upon return to his or her job. You could say that the further up in the hierarchy the employee is, the more emphasis there should be on business awareness training and managerial skills up-date.

During the training session—particularly the management sessions—you should personally make a point of being a presenter. You should present the company's strategy, situation, important issues etc. There are very few occasions where you get better contact with your people than during such training sessions.

Appraisal and Counselling (Performance Reviews)

You should also establish an Appraisal and Counseling system in which the managers and their direct reports—at least annually, but ideally more often—establish goals for their subordinates and review their performance regularly. This should start at the top where the chairman has such a session with the General Manager. The General Manager has it with his direct reports—the functional managers. The functional managers have such meetings with their direct reports etc. There are numerous books on this subject and I will not go deeply into this at this time. The only thing that I want to stress is that you should establish concrete, measurable goals applicable to the next period. After the initial period is over you should start with an evaluation of the performance for the past period. You should determine what went well and identify areas where the employee needs to improve. After this conversation you should establish performance criteria (goals) for the forthcoming period. Try to establish a meeting with a good atmosphere and handle conflict so that both parties come out as winners. However, from time to time, the performance of an employee may be substandard. Then it is the responsibility of the manager to take the proper corrective actions. First of all, you should attempt to improve his performance in his current job. If that does not work, you may transfer the individual to another job in a different department. If that does not work, you might have to separate him from the company. Again, every time that you have meetings of this nature you should try to maintain the individual's dignity. Here I would like to quote Chairman Mao again. In the following he sums up the content of appraisal and counseling:

We must know how to take good care of the cadres (employees). There are several ways of doing so.

First, *give them guidance. This means allowing them a free hand in their works so that they have the courage to assume responsibility and, at the same time giving them timely instructions so that, guided by the party's political line, they are able to make full use of their initiative.*

Second, *raise their level. This means educating them by giving them the opportunity to study so that they can enhance their theoretical understanding and their working ability.*

Third, *check up on their work, and help them sum up their experience, carry forward their achievements and correct their mistakes. To assign work without checking up and to take notice only when serious mistakes are made—that is not the way to take care of cadres.*

Fourth, *in general use the method of persuasion with cadres who have made mistakes, and help them to correct their mistakes. The method of struggle should be confined to those who make serious mistakes and nevertheless refuse to accept the* *guidance. Here patience is essential. It is wrong lightly to label people "opportunists" or lightly to begin "waging" struggle against them.*

Fifth, *help them with their difficulties. When cadres are in difficulty as a result of illness, straitened means, or domestic or other trouble, we must be sure to give them as much care as possible.*

This is to take good care of cadres (employees).

I am convinced that if more companies handled their employees in the spirit of this quotation, there would be much higher productivity, more loyalty, a higher morale, more satisfied employees etc. in corporate life all over the world. In this quotation Chairman Mao ingeniously demonstrates his altruism as far as managerial skills are concerned.

Many companies have designed forms where the Appraisal and Counseling discussions are recorded and the goals documented.

In the beginning, new managers often find it difficult to play this role. However, after training and some practical experience, he or she will be more comfortable with setting goals, assessing the performance of their subordinates and using this important tool for company development. After all, humans want to have feedback on their performance.

Role model

As the head of the company, you will be a person that everybody looks up to. If you want the organization to focus on service quality, you have to do it yourself. If you want people to take advantage of the possibilities that the IT-technology offers, you have to demonstrate that you use the tools yourself. If you want people to be honest with their travel expenses, you will have to be honest yourself. Remember that your moves and steps are being followed and you are being scrutinized, judged, evaluated every day. Make sure that you can stand the test every time. That is the only way to earn their respect and loyalty which are very important prerequisites for the success of your company. Be a good listener. Many executives have an ego that results in them speaking all the time. It is boring to listen to one's own opinions. In my mind it is much more interesting to listen to what other people have to say. You should also show compassion when some of your employees are hit with an unfortunate situation in life—i.e. become ill, lose a loved one, are part in an accident, must change jobs etc. I refer to the fifth way of taking good care of cadres above.

I have read a couple of good articles about behavior that is not desirable for executives and I would like to cite them for you. The first appeared in *Business Week* on April 1, 1991 and was titled "Does your Boss have it?".

Its subtitle is CEO disease—egotism can breed corporate disaster and the malady is spreading. Although this article is somewhat old, I believe its issues are still very valid. The traits of the malady are the following

# 1	# 2	# 3	# 4
He and she can do no wrong, refusing to concede any mistake.	*Spends excessive time on the boards of other companies or civic groups playing the role of a statesman*	*Surrounded by sycophants who yes the boss' every whim*	*Wants to make every decision, but doesn't bother finding out all the details*
# 5	**# 6**	**# 7**	**# 8**
Always trying to be one up on counterparts in salary, headquarters, aircraft	*Overly concerned about where she sits in meetings or whether people rise when he enters a room.*	*Relishes media attention – not especially for the company, but for personal gain*	*Hangs on to the job too long – often undermining candidates who might someday be successors*

Make sure that you as a manager are not labelled with these types of characteristics and rather let the following statements that also were part of the article make sure that you avoid the pitfalls of power:

- No yes-men
- Impose limits on the job's perks (perk = privileges beyond salaries, liked cars, aircraft, lavish offices, excessive entertainment account etc.)
- Stay focused on the job itself
- Don't assume that toughness defines leadership
- Keep the communication channels open

An other article that I fancy very much was written by Sydney Finkelstein in the January/February 2004 edition of *Ivey Business Journal*. It was titled **"The seven habits of spectacularly unsuccessful executives."** This article points at seven highly dangerous traits of the personality portfolio of executives and all of them should be avoided at any price. Below I have pulled together the main points of the article by describing what the negative trait is, what kind of signals that they convey to their colleagues, subordinates, customers and other stakeholders. I believe that they are pretty self-explanatory and that you clearly understand that you should avoid this type of behavior.

Habit # 1: They see themselves and their companies as dominating their environment
Warning sign: A lack of respect
Thoughts in their minds: "Our products are superior, so am I.—We're untouchable. My company is successful because of my leadership and intellect—I made it happen."

Habit # 2: They identify so completely with the company that there is no clear boundary between their personal interests and their corporation's interest.
Warning sign: A question of character.
Thoughts in their minds: "I am the sole proprietor. This is my baby. Obviously, my wants and needs are in the best interest of my company and stockholders."

Habit # 3: They think they have all the answers.
Warning sign: A leader without followers.
Thoughts in their minds: "I'm a genius. I believe in myself and you should too. Don't worry, I know all the answers. I'm not micro-managing; I'm being attentive. I don't need anybody else, certainly not a team."

Habit # 4: They ruthlessly eliminate anyone who isn't completely behind them
Warning sign: Executive departures.

Thoughts in their minds: "If you are not with me, you're against me. Get with the plan, or get out of the way. Where's your loyalty."

Habit # 5: They are consummate spokespersons, obsessed with the company image.
Warning sign: Blatant attention-seeking
Thoughts in their minds: "I'm the spokesperson. It's all about image. I'm a promotions and public relations genius. I love making public appearances: that's why I star in our commercial. It is my job to be socially visible; that's why I give speeches and have a regular media coverage."

Habit # 6: They underestimate the obstacles
Warning sign: Excessive hype
Thoughts in their minds: "It's just a minor roadblock. Full steam ahead! Let's call that division in a "partner company" so that we don't have to show it on our books."

Habit # 7: They stubbornly rely on what worked for them in the past
Warning sign: Constantly referring to what worked in the past.
Thoughts in their minds: "It has always worked this way in the past. We've done it before, and we can do it again."

Source: "The seven habits of spectacularly unsuccessful executives" by Sidney Finkelstein—*Ivey Business Journal*, published by Ivey publishing, The University of Western Ontario.

Mr. Finkelstein brightly points out the following in closing the article: *"These seven habits of spectacularly unsuccessful people are powerful reminders of how organizational leaders are not only instruments of growth and success, but sometimes also the architects of failure. That each of the habits have elements that are valuable for leaders only serves to point out how vigilant people who enter a leader's orbit must be, whether they are other executives, board members, lower-level managers and employees, regulators, or even suppliers, customers and competitors. In small doses each of the habits can be part of a winning formula, but when executives overdose, the habit can quickly become toxic. That is a lesson all leaders and would-be leaders should take to the heart".*

Design and Branding

You may think that it is odd, but design and branding might be one of the most important weapons that a company has at its disposal in the fight for customers and attention from the environment. I address this under the General Manager section because I consider it to be an extremely important part of a company's identity. Through design and branding you have a tremendous ability to distinguish yourself and stand out in comparison with your competitors. Today, most products are generic and easy to copy. The technology that is used in your products is more or less the same technology that is used by your competitors and if not the properties are basically the same. So you have to create your own corporate identity, brand names, designs, logos etc. Look at the PC-industry. Most of the brands have "Intel Inside". This is the situation that you find in many other industries—so there is a need for making sure that your product is getting its place in the sun.

An important tool for attaining this is the emotional value that you can attach to your products and services. Let me give you a few examples:

- This morning I called my cell phone operator. Before I called them I was somewhat irritated because something had happened that was very unpleasant and impractical for me. So I was prepared to really give them hell. However, the most charming customer representative took my call. He immediately took care of the problem and within minutes my anger was turned into a pleasant conversation with a person who sat there at the other end of the telephone line with the only objective of making me—Mr. Customer—happy. And he did. How do you think that I will react the next time one of this company's competitors calls me to have me change cell phone operator?
- The other day I read in the newspaper that a company producing and marketing vodka had changed the design of their bottle and labels. Suddenly—almost with no marketing effort—sales had doubled.

- Some time ago I learned about a company in Switzerland. They imported salmon from Norway at a price of 6 dollars a kilo. This company brought it into the Swiss alps where the salmon was smoked in a special way, put on a little wooden tray after being sliced, then put under cellophane together with a spoonful of Russian caviar. Then it was called "Czar Nicolai's filets" and sold in the most luxurious food stores in Paris, Geneva, London etc. Can you believe it—the price was now 200 dollars per kilo. Yes, you heard correctly—200 dollars—about thirty times more expensive than the raw fish that was imported from Norway. Why was that? The salmon had been refined and worked up, given a fancy name, a different packaging and it was distributed through channels where they hit the right customers. This warrants what we call a premium price.

Think about Coca Cola (beverage), Mercedes Benz (cars), Gucci (fashion), Dior (fashion), McDonalds (fast food); Sony (electronics), Nokia (mobile telephones), Singapore Airlines (transportation), American Express (financial services), Boss (men's clothing), Nike (sporting garments), IKEA (furniture); Absolut (vodka) and a number of other brand names. In their respective fields they are all basically selling the same functions and benefits as their competitors. However, there are particular reasons why they are more attractive than their competitors. There are some emotional values attached to their products and services through their logo, brand, design, service delivery, quality or perceived quality, snob value, price, the customers that they want to appeal to and of course functionality. These emotional values and certainly many others are very decisive for the choices that their customers are making and the price that they are willing to pay. The more solidly these emotional values are embedded in the minds of the prospective customers, the higher the price that they are willing to pay—in other words, they are willing to pay the premium price despite the fact that the quality and functionality of a competitive product exists that is less expensive than their own.

Countries and companies with a finished goods product range have a significant advantage over countries and companies that are selling raw materials. The disadvantage is that the price of such products is created in a world market, where there are many suppliers and each supplier's products are almost the same as the other suppliers. Therefore, you must attach features to your products that distinguish them from other similar products. If your product line is close to raw materials or other generic products, a premium price element may be warranted through customer service, delivery lead times, sales conditions, reliability etc.

I cannot stress sufficiently how crucial this point is.

Private life

Remember also that it is important for a president, general manager or top executive to have a full life. Many of the most successful executives have a hobby where they get a different type of experience. Many of them are good at following up their children by being well informed about their schoolwork, attending their ballgames, their music lessons and other extracurricular activities. They work normal hours when they are not out traveling and try to recharge their batteries by taking their vacations. This does not preclude them from working around the clock when that is required to handle a crisis, to complete a tender before a deadline or something similar.

You should be well informed about politics and what is going on in the society around you. The sources for this are newspapers, magazines, TV-viewing, radio-listening, the internet etc.

It does not hurt to read books with subjects that are far removed from your daily work. Literature widens your horizon and improves your ability to understand things profoundly, philosophically and from a historical point of view.

And, why not take a stint with local community work. This brings you out among common people and through contact with them you have an opportunity to understand people at levels in society that are below your own. Do a part of your socializing with people that do not belong to your own social group—that do not work in business, that do not work in the same line of business as yourself, that have an education that is entirely different than your own, that come from other parts of the world or of the company. In this context remember what Chairman Mao said:

> *Pay attention to uniting and working with comrades who differ with you. This should be borne in mind in the localities and in the army. It also applies to the relations with people outside the Party. We have*

come together from every corner of the country and should be good at
uniting in our work and not only with comrades who hold the same
views as we but also with those who hold different views.

In a final note I would also like to quote another important Chinese
leader, Lao Tsu, who lived many, many years ago. He said:

"Superior leaders get things done with very little motion. They impart
instruction not through many words, but through a few deeds. They
keep informed about everything but interfere hardly at all. They are
catalysts, and though things would not get done as well if they were not
there, when they succeed they take no credit. And, because they take no
credit, credit never leaves them".

As a leader of any type of organization one should also note what this
ancient hero says about the subject of being a leader. His words are as valid
today as they were when he lived in the *6th century B.C.,*

VI

Other Considerations

We should be modest and prudent, guard against arrogance and rashness, and serve the Chinese people heart and soul . . . .

"China's Two Possible Destinies" (April 23, 1945),
Selected Works, Vol. III, p. 253. LRB 170.

We must never adopt an arrogant attitude of great-power chauvinism and become conceited because of the victory of our revolution and certain achievements in our construction. Every nation—big or small—has its weak points.

"Opening Address at the Eighth National Congress of the
Communist Party of China" (September 15, 1956). LRB 180.

Even if we achieve gigantic successes in our work, there is no reason whatsoever to fell conceited and arrogant. Modesty helps one to get forwards whereas conceit makes one lag behind. This is a truth that we must always bear in mind.

"Opening Address at the Eight National Congress of the
Communist Party of China" (September 11, 1956). LRB 237.

With victory, certain moods may grow within the Party—arrogance, the airs of a self-styled hero, inertia, and unwillingness to make progress, love of pleasure and distaste for continued hard living. With victory, the people will be grateful to us and the bourgeoisie will come forward to flatter us. It has been proved that the enemy cannot conquer us by force of arms. However, the flattery of the bourgeoisies may conquer the weak-willed in our ranks. There may be some Communists, who were not conquered by enemies with guns and were worthy of the names of heroes for standing up to these enemies, but cannot withstand sugar-coated bullets; they will be defeated by sugar-coated bullets. We must guard against such a situation.

"Report to the Second Plenary Session of the Seventh Central
Committee of the Communist Party of China" (March 5, 1949)
Selected Works, Vol. IV. p. 374. LRB 237.

Business Ethics

While businesses in the past could be run secretively, with reduced public insight, the power in the hands of "The Old Boys' Network", unhealthy monopolies and cartels, disrespect for the dignity of the workers, abuse of power by owners and management, tax evasion, corruption, bribes and illegal kick-backs, non-commercial considerations when decisions were taken, nepotism in hiring and promotion situations, transfer pricing, incorporation in tax heavens, ignorance of national and international laws, rules and regulations, exploitation of third country human and natural resources—the situation today is entirely different. And that is good.

Today the responsibilities of the board are greater and more visible; the auditors can be brought to justice if they are not honest in their evaluations, national and international data systems facilitate monitoring and tracing of transactions, the press is more independent and inquisitive than in the past; the laws are tougher, the public opinion has a different slant; the employees have stronger rights than what they used to have, consumer groups and consumerism have a strong position and we have organizations like Green Peace and Attack to mention a few reasons for this development. The consumers—who after all are paying our paychecks—are holding the corporations accountable for their products and the way in which they are marketed. Consumers are looking for brand values that mean product performance and real product benefits. It is also very important to keep these principles in high esteem even when facing a difficult economic climate or other types of risk. Unfortunately, many business leaders believe that some of these factors are hinderances rather than positive catalysts in the development of their company and only pay lip service to these factors. You might get a short gain by ignoring some of these points but in the long run it is healthy for business development to observe these rules, which are very reasonable in the type of societies that we—fortunately—now are developing where there is much more democracy, little acceptance for illegalities and where one strong man no longer can have the single-handed authority to do what he wants.

There is a wave over the western world that emphasizes ethical behavior in corporate life. When you study the values, visions and cultural traits of western corporations today you will see that they emphasize the existence of ethical principles in the way they want to profile themselves for their staff, but also for the external environment. It is a great belief that ethical conduct is good for business and that it improves the results since other businesses want to deal with honest partners who act with integrity and honesty in all their business dealings whether they are customers, staff, suppliers, neighbors, stockholders etc. Very often such values can be tracked back to the founders who were committed to business ethics and corporate responsibility. There are numerous examples of this.

The head of a company is responsible for articulating the values and being a role model who continuously demonstrates to the environment that he is holding these principles in high esteem and that he is holding his direct reports responsible for the same. "Walk the talk" is an American expression. What it means is practice what you preach—be a role model.

You must realize that being successful in business goes hand in hand with business ethics and social responsibility. The values and the conduct of a company should be among the sources of its reputation.

When you work with ethics, there are three basic questions to be raised:

- Is it legal?
- Is it reasonable?
- Is it right?

Most of us will require our company to comply with the laws of the country and demand that the employees do the same. However, within the boundaries of what is legal it is possible for the company to establish rules for what is reasonable. Something that is legally ok is—for many reasons—not necessarily reasonable. These reasons could relate to the reputation and position of the company, the society where the company is residing, the history of the company etc. Furthermore, within the boundaries of what is legal and reasonable, we may question whether it is right. Here we are talking about our ethical attitudes and personal morale, our self-esteem and our own perceptions of what is right or wrong. Very often companies hire top-notch lawyers who have no difficulty defending and articulating that a certain action is legally correct according to the book. However, in the eyes of society, the employees, the stockholders and other interested parties, a certain action might not be perceived as reasonable and right. Often I am surprised to see super-intelligent corporate officers contend that since a particular situation is legal it is also reasonable and right. My point is that this is not necessarily correct. In a matter like this it is easier to "sweep the broom in front of somebody else's door than one's own"—to use an old Norwegian saying.

As I write this part of the book, I read in the local business paper that the top management of a very successful international Norwegian company has been accused by the Stock Exchange Control Authorities for questionable trading in the company's shares. What they did was in a legal grey zone and they were not persecuted. However, the legal boundaries did not necessarily draw the line between what is right and what is wrong for business managers who wanted to maintain a good reputation. What draws the line is what is perceived as reasonable.

I remember a well-known executive who was interviewed about business conduct. He said that the worst thing that he could think of was a negative article in the morning newspaper about his conduct that hit his children right in the face around the breakfast table. I think this is a good guidance for behaviour and you should probably add your employees and their children to the list as well.

The view at the top must be that ethics are extremely important for the well-being of an organization. If you as a top executive do something unethical to benefit yourself or the company, how can you build credibility with your staff? No matter how large the financial or other gain from an unethical deed is, there is "a price" when employees witness that their superiors cross boundaries in ethical questions. In today's transparent world this will be more and more prevalent.

On a final note I would like to commend large corporations—particularly the American—for the positive impact that they have had on my attitudes about business ethics. During my years with IBM I learned a lot about ethical behavior. IBM had an undisputable attitude in such matters. They issued annually a little booklet called "Business Conduct Guidelines". This was a document that all the staff with external contacts—like sales personnel, purchasing representatives and service engineers had to read every year in order to reinforce good behaviour. In the copy that I hold in my hands the main chapters were:

- *IBM's Business Principles*
- *Compliance with the Anti-trust laws*
- *Business Ethics including*

  - *Customer Relations*
  - *Supplier Relations*
  - *Financial Interests in Competitive Companies*
  - *Use of own time*
  - *Incorrect use of Internal Information*
  - *Conflicts of Interest of non-personal character*

This booklet was a guiding torch for the IBM representatives in their dealings—particularly with the outside world—and I am certain that it saved people a lot of time and the organization a lot of "damage repair" in the aftermath of non-businesslike behavior that otherwise would have happened.

Please take this seriously. You might lose a few wins in the short perspective—but in the long run you gain financially as well as personally from being a lighthouse for your employees in ethical questions. Make sure that high ethical standards are important ingredients of your corporate culture. Also, listen to the "whistle-blowers", e.g. create a climate at the work places, where it is perfectly legitimate for any employee to voice issues of a questionable and critical nature.

Crisis Management

A crisis can happen in any company, anytime, anywhere and although you consider the risk limited you should be prepared to handle a crisis that is developing.

Let us have a look at the type of crises that you can be exposed to in a relatively normal business. They could be: accidents, airplane crashes, explosions, food contamination, fire, kidnapping, storms, abnormal heat or other damaging weather conditions, industrial accidents, earthquakes, negative financial results, lay-offs, motor vehicle accidents, emission of toxic water, air and other waste, robbery, suicide, sabotage, threats, death of a colleague etc. The nature of your business will determine where the risks are and what kind of preparedness to handle "the unthinkable" is required.

Most companies have programs in place to prevent things from happening and sketchy plans for how to handle an accident, disaster or other unexpected events. What I would like to stress is that this is not a matter of administration only. Crisis normally also have an impact on human beings. They often lead to great emotional stress and it is very important that you as a company executive are able to cope with the stress symptoms. As the head of the helicopter company I experienced a fatal accident. First, the three customers and a pilot of the aircraft were missing for ten hours. The search and rescue were hampered by bad weather conditions. Finally, we learned that two of the three passengers were killed. The surviving passenger—a seven-year-old boy—was the son of one of the deceased and the nephew of the other. We gained a lot of respect by showing empathy and compassion for the deceased and their families in addition to taking good care of the pilot's relatives before we had the technical talk on national TV, in the newspapers, in the local communities, to the employees. Fortunately, I had had emergency training as an executive in an airline and in a cruise-ferry company prior to this accident. Through that training we gained a lot of knowledge about the way things like this should be handled from an administrative as well as a human perspective. I want to emphasize how traumatizing unexpected negative events can be for people. Therefore, in connection with a crisis make sure that you address personal and emotional dimensions as well as the technical aspects.

It is very difficult to be general on such a theme, but what I recommend is that you together with your colleagues brainstorm to disclose what your risks for crises are and design the programs that are required to handle this in case the unexpected happens—including training of your people so that everybody knows his or her role when such things occur.

Media and Public Attention.

As a business executive you may get a lot of attention from the press. They will be interested in financial results, plans, new product announcements, new hires and promotions, new locations, conflicts that you may have with suppliers, competitors etc., strikes and labor disputes, downsizing of staff, closing of administrative or production sites, accidents, you as a head of the company, your stock prices, your reaction to what others have expressed, and things that demonstrate that the press live up to their desire to be inquisitive and critical.

Maintain an open and honest tone. Do not try to conceal things that will come to the surface sooner or later in any case. There are some who will say: *"Always be honest in your replies, but also remember that you do not have to tell everything"*. Treat the press with respect and try to be responsive, but by the same token be aware of your rights. F. ex., you are not obliged to answer any questions at any time. If you get a call from a journalist, tell him that you will call him back at a certain time. This is important if you have to get more information about the matter before you want to be interviewed or if you want to buy yourself some time before you "get into the heat". Remember that the journalists have a job to do and you can help them to do their job as well as possible.

Make sure that you also take the initiative for contact with the press. Make your company available for the press, be an ambassador for your industry and contribute with information about development, trends, products, technologies etc. It is important that the journalists and the newspapers, the TV-company etc. know who they should contact in your company. If they know such details in advance they will not waste their own time and you will be certain that they are talking to the right person—the person who knows all the facts and the total background.

Arrange press conferences from time to time. But remember that the press will not play the role of a "microphone rack" where you are allowed to tell your story without being able to ask critical questions. You should always have a real story or piece of news to tell them when you call a press conference. Do not expect them to print your message unedited. They will try to find their own angle and you have to respect that.

When you are exposed to the attention of the press for the first time, you will want to see what they have written before it is printed. This is a right that you have. You can require an amendment if you feel that you have not been quoted correctly or if there are factual errors in the article. Their opinions and judgements you cannot ask them to change. My experience has been that after a while you become relaxed and are not too anxious to approve every word of an article. I personally think that this is best. Therefore, do not waste your time by reading and changing everything before printing.

Appearance on TV is becoming more and more common. This is a ball game that is different compared to an interview for a newspaper article. My advice when you are new to this is that you (of course) prepare yourself very well, answer in short sentences and let the interviewer follow on with new questions. As you become more seasoned and experienced, you can try to take control over the situation.

If it is likely that you will be exposed to press attention frequently, I would advise you to arrange a Media-Training Course where you hire a consultant—normally a journalist, an editor or such—to train you and your staff to be able to meet the media in a credible way. If you become involved in an accident with casualties, a severe emission of toxic waste, a claim from a competitor or something similar, a lot of unnecessary damage to you and your company can be avoided if you are able to meet the media in the right way. There are numerous examples where people have tried to avoid the truth in the beginning, but have been caught severely when the facts that they presented initially were inconsistent with the real truth. The Enron case from the beginning of 2002 is such a case. The management started to lie and all of a sudden they were entangled in a web of false information that they were not able to get out of. Then the snowball started to roll and they found themselves in a completely uncontrolled and uncontrollable situation.

Best Without Ball and Other Things
We Could Learn From the Sports World

What Did Mao say?

You have many good qualities and having rendered great service, but you must always remember not to become conceited. You are respected by all, and quite rightly, but this easily leads to conceit. If you become conceited, if you are not modest and cease to exert yourselves, and if you do not respect others, do not respect the cadres and the masses, then you will cease to be heroes and models. There have been such people in the past, and I hope you will not follow their example.

"We Must Learn to Do Economic Work" (January 10, 1945)
Selected Works, Vol. III, p. 139. LRB 183.

Don't wait until problems pile up and cause a lot of trouble before trying to solve them. Leaders must march ahead of the movement, and not lag behind it.

Introductory note to "Contract on a Seasonal Basis" (1955)
The Upsurge in China's Countryside, Chinese ed., Vol. III. LRB 229.

In the sports world athletes are very goal-oriented and very often business can learn a lot from their efforts to become winners. In Norway we had a coach for the national team in soccer by the name of "Drillo" or Egil Olsen. He was the first professor in soccer in Norway and as such he was a very analytical person. He recorded all matches on video and after the game he carefully reviewed them, found the weak and strong points of the team, and used that to improve the tactics and strategies for the next game. Before important matches he filmed the opponents during their last games before they were supposed to meet Norway and used this to decide on the tactics to be applied.

One of the things he found out was that in an average match each player on the average is in contact with the ball for about three minutes. This meant that each player had 87 minutes of the match in which they did not have anything to do. As a result of this, he invented the term "best without ball". What he meant was that it was extremely important to do something during these 87 minutes without the ball that moved the play forward in favor of one's own team. I learned about this principle during the world championship in France—where the Norwegian National Team was one of the play-off teams.

I thought that it was such an interesting philosophy that it could be usefully applied to the working life. My analysis had shown me that all employees have periods where they are "without the ball" in the sense that they do nothing important for the company or themselves. I said to myself that during these periods the employees should be trained to ask themselves: "What can I do to move the company or myself forward?"

I urged my employees to ask themselves this question when they were idle and I soon found out that they had this in mind and tried to apply it to their particular situation. An example of this is as follows. During my tenure in the helicopter company the pilots were waiting for ambulance mission or they were grounded due to bad weather conditions. Consequently, they had a lot of time where they had nothing to do while they were waiting for a call from the Emergency Call Center. For them to be "best without the ball" could be to sweep the hangar floors or read manuals regarding technical updates of the aircraft. All the employees were given a CD-Rom that contained courses that brought them forward to a test in their Information Technology aptitudes. To be "best without ball" for them was to go through a few sections of this training program. In other contexts this could be to read professional and business magazines, surf on the Internet for job-related subjects and thus update job-skills and competence. On commending employees for an extraordinary effort I remember that many of them said thanks with the following words: "You remember—best without ball".

"To take responsibility" was a term that a female coach—Marit Breivik—for the Norwegian Ladies National Team in handball used. They were one of the best teams in the world for many years and she induced in the players a sense of responsibility that made each of them do more than their best. In business life this is called empowering. Marit and the Norwegian team won the goldmedal in the 2008 Olympic Games in Beijing.

There are many other traits of the winning culture that you find in the sports world that you could try to foster in your employees. Discipline, endurance, persistence, teamwork, tactics, planning, and strategy are a few key words that are necessary for men or women to be successful in sports. I believe that the same words are important for being successful in business.

Invite successful sportsmen and women to meet your management and your employees. Ask them to tell you how they plan their training, how they motivate themselves to do their utmost during competitions when it is necessary to be physically as well as mentally strong and other important things that make them winners.

Youth

What Did Mao say?

The world is yours, as well as ours, but in the last analysis it is yours. You young people, full of vigour and vitality, are in the bloom of life, like the sun at eight or nine in the morning. Our hope is placed on you . . . . The World belongs to you. China's future belongs to you.

Talk at a Greeting with Chinese Students and Trainees in Moscow—
November 17, 1957. LRB 288.

We must help all our young people to understand that ours is still a very poor country, that we cannot change this situation radically in a short time, and that only through the united efforts of our younger generation and all our people, working with their own hands, can China be made strong and prosperous within a period of several decades. The establishment of our socialist system has opened the road leading to the ideal society of the future, but to translate this ideal into reality needs hard work.

On the Correct Handling of Contradictions Among the People
(February 27, 1957), 1st Pocket Edition, pp. 44-45. LRB 288

Because of their lack of political and social experience, quite a number of young people are unable to see the contrast between the old China and the new, and it is not easy for them to comprehend the hardships our people went through in the struggle to free themselves from the oppression of the imperialists and Kuomintang reactionaries, or the long period of arduous work needed before a happy socialist society can be established. That is why we must constantly carry on lively and effective political education among the masses and should always tell them the truth about the difficulties that crop up and discuss with them how to surmount these difficulties.

"On the Correct Handling of Contradictions Among the People"
(February 27, 1957), 1st Pocket Edition, p. 64. LRB 289.

The young people are the most active and vital force in society. They are the most eager to learn and the least conservative in their thinking. This is especially so in the area of socialism. We hope that the local Party Organizations in various places will help and work with the Youth League organizations and go into the question of bringing into full play the energy of the youth in particular. The Party organizations should not treat them in the same way as everybody else and ignore their special characteristics. Of course, the young people should learn from the old and other adults, and should strive as much as possible to engage in all sorts of useful activities with their agreements.

Introductory note to "a Youth Shock Brigade of the no. 9 Agricultural Producers's Co-operative in Hsinping Township, Chuangthan County" (1955), The Socialist Upsurge in Chinas's Countryside. Chinese ed., Vol. III. LRB 291.

For all companies it is necessary to recruit young people who can become tomorrow's management and professionals. It is also important to focus on increasing the ability of the company to quickly develop and exploit the total knowledge of the company in a way that increases earnings and reduces cost and expenses. A similar objective is to create an exciting work environment and ensure that the employees are sharing their knowledge and competence with each other.

When the new hires are coming on board, they should attend an introduction course of a day or two. During such lessons they should learn about important aspects of their new employer, which puts them in a position to function as quickly as possible in their jobs. The curriculum should consist of matters of administrative character as well as business dynamics and the missions and values of the company. All new employees should attend these courses so that they understand the administrative framework of the company, its history, its product line and other important matters. If feasible, I would recommend that a person from higher management gives a presentation with his or her perspective in mind. That is always very much appreciated by such groups of "unsung heroes", as one of my bosses in IBM characterized them.

The immediate manager and the newly recruited person should have a meeting after two to three weeks to agree on a position description that broadly outlines what the job consists of, to whom the position reports, what the responsibilities are and what authority the incumbent has and what the employee is authorized to do independently. Such a meeting should result in a written document in which these important things are stated. In addition, they should also agree on a set of objectives for the first period of employment. As I have stated several times the way a new employee is received from day one and is treated throughout his or her entire time in the company, is extremely important for that person's satisfaction with the company. Hiring the wrong person is extremely expensive and to make the person the right person, the company also has to take the responsibility for integrating him as quickly and as well as possible.

Most corporations should have a program insuring that the company in the short and long run has the competence and capabilities that are needed to take care of today's business and develop it to meet the challenges of the future. I would advise you to establish a program for this—like they do in IBM, Hewlett Packard, Exxon and other orderly-run companies. In IBM there was a term called "vitality hiring". The purpose of this was to ensure that the companies had a sufficient amount of young employees that they could develop into the positions mentioned above. That meant that—irrespective of financial conditions—they hired a certain number of promising university graduates every year and sent them through sales- and marketing training, engineering training, vocational training, financial training and other programs that ensured that the company at any time had the resources that were required to fill the various positions.

The same is the purpose of trainee programs more and more companies establish. The purpose of these types of programs is also a certain degree of "indoctrination," since they also introduce the participants to the mission, visions, values and culture of the company. Furthermore, the training will aim at giving the trainees an insight into the financial dynamics and the forces that impact the situation of the company. For a newly arrived employee this is very useful information, but it is also motivating and creates loyalty—a loyalty that is very important to attain since in this group you will find those of your employees that are most apt to leave since they do not have all the information that is required to understand what kind of company they are working for.

Women and Minorities

What Did Mao say?

Unite and take part in the production and political activity to improve the economic and political status of women.

Inscription for the magazine "Women in New China",
printed in its first issue, July 20, 1949. LRB 296.

Protect the interests of the youth, women and children—provide assistance to young student refugees, help the youth and women to organize in order to participate on an equal footing in all work useful to the war effort and to social progress, ensure freedom of marriage and equality as between men and women and give young people and children a useful education.

"On Coalition Government" (April 24, 1945).
Selected Works. Vol. III, p. 188. LRB 296.

In . . . . production our fundamental task is to adjust the use of labour power in an organized way and to encourage women to do . . . . work.

"Our Economic Policy" (January 23, 1934).
Selected Works, Vol. I, p. 188. LRB 296.

In order to build a great socialist society, it is of the utmost importance to arouse the broad masses of women to join in productive activity. Men and women must receive equal pay for equal work in production activity. Genuine equality between the sexes can only be realized in the process of the socialist transformation of society as a whole.

Introductory note to "Women Have Gone to the Labour Front" (1955),
The Socialist Upsurge in China's Countryside,
Chinese ed., Vol. I. LRB 297.

> *With the completion of agricultural co-operation, many co-operatives are finding themselves short of labour. It has become necessary to arouse the great mass women who did not work in the fields before to take their place on the labour front . . . China's women are a vast reserve of labour power. This reserve should be tapped in the struggle to build a great socialist country.*
>
> Introductory note to "Solving the Labour Shortage by Arousing the Women to Join in the Production" (1955), The Sosialist Upsurge in Chinas' Countryside. Chinese ed, Vol. I. LRB 298.
>
> *Enable every woman who can work to take her place on the labour front under the principle of equal pay for equal work. This should be done as quickly as possible.*
>
> Introductory note to "On Widening the Scope of Women's Work in the Agricultural Co-operative Movement" (1955), The Sosialist Upsurge in Chinas' Countryside. Chinese ed., Vol. I. LRB 298.
>
> *Pay attention to uniting and working with comrades who differ with you. This should be borne in mind in the localities and in the army. It also applies to the relations with people outside the Party. We have come together from every corner of the country and should be good at uniting in our work and not only with comrades who hold the same views as we but also with those who hold different views.*
>
> "Methods of Workof Party Committees" March 13, 1949), Vol. IV, p. 377. LRB 113.
>
> *Take the ideas of the masses and concentrate them, then go to the masses, persevere in the ideas and carry them through, so as to form correct ideas of leadership—such is the basic method of leadership.*
>
> "Some Questions Concerning Methods of Leadership" (June 1, 1943), Selected Works, Vol. III, p. 120. LRB 128.

Equal opportunity for men and women is a corporate objective that has prevailed in western business for two to three decades. Although there is a lot of focus on this, there are many people who are disappointed with the progress and claim that we have not come as far as we should. In this perspective, it is extremely interesting to read Chairman Mao's thoughts on this and how strongly he urged that one took advantage of the other half of the population, not only as willing hands to do productive work, but also to use the vast intellectual capacity that the women represent. Nowadays there is an entirely different attitude towards women and other minorities compared to what it was a few years ago. Today you find females in presidential positions in large corporations and in managerial positions in corporations as well as in politics and civic life.

It is interesting to note when Mao made his points about women. It took place in a period that went from the 1930's to the 1950's and 60's. If western business society—as well as society at large—had been equally interested at that time to engage the force of the women in work and political life, I am certain that the world would have been very different and that the history of the twentieth century would have been written differently than what it actually was. Today, it is natural for women to fill high positions in the work force.

To gain the maximum out of the influx of women in leading positions, it is important to allow women to be women with their approach and reactions to things and not encourage them to be clones of men. In the beginning, women in such positions tried to imitate men in the way that they dressed and behaved. Today it is different. They populate corporate life as women and there is no doubt that they make an impact with their background and opinions when their style is driven by their particular female traits.

However, despite the strong focus on their entry into the work force, I believe that there are many who would say that progress has not been good enough. Statistically at least that is a fact. Still, there are very few women in top positions as general managers, company presidents and in the board rooms. Many would say that this is due to an antagonistic attitude among men towards women in such jobs. Many believe that they do not have the stamina and persistence that is required to fill such positions, they are more absent because they have more responsibility for the care of children and their homes, they are not willing to take the strain of late nights and much travel etc. Many men probably have such attitudes. However, I think that often women are more inclined to evaluate what the job will require and on a very rational evaluation they say that this type of job is not for me. Very often women—as opposed to men—will say that I am not able to succeed in such a job, while men will have fewer doubts about their own qualifications.

In some countries there are strong movements to increase the share of women with so-called "positive discrimination". This means if there are two candidates—a man and a women—with equal competence the woman should be preferred. In Norway there is a practice to fill the ministerial posts in the Government with at least 40% women and there are political intentions to make it mandatory to have a similar ratio of women in the corporate board rooms. Personally, I believe that this is a disservice to women. They should be appointed to managerial jobs and board positions with the basis in their qualifications and not because of gender. That, however, does not mean that we should not focus on the opportunities that are inherent in making sure that women are employed and that we rid society of stupid opinions about the abilities and attitudes of women.

In the United States there is a strong focus on three terms—sexism, sexual harassment and sexual discrimination and there are strong penalties for individuals as well as for corporations when there are violations of the law in these areas. *Sexism*—briefly explained—is to have posters, calendars etc. on the walls with nude or close-to-nude women. The use of slanderous language is also an example of sexism. *Sexual harassment* is unconsented advances with sexual activities in mind or to take advantage of a powerful position to obtain sexual favors, while *sexual discrimination* is to let gender be a decisive factor for or against employment and promotion to higher positions.

I also believe that there is a vast reserve—intellectually and as hard-working members of the work force—in migrant workers and handicapped individuals. However, many places—not the least in my country and my part of the world—there is resistance towards hiring and promoting people with unusual (foreign) names, a different color and with physical or other handicaps. This is a shame as well as a waste, and I urge you to drop your preconceived notions—if you have any—and treat these groups and women with the same respect and dignity as men without handicaps. You will get a nicer work climate, you will increase your productivity and you will get the type of versatility in the company that fosters creativity, innovation and cooperation. You will also be better positioned to sell your products to the entire population when you have employees with handicaps or are amongst minorities that can advise you on how to approach them with your marketing message.

VII

Final Notes

What Did Mao Say?

The history of mankind is one of continuous development from the realm of necessity to the realm of freedom. This process is never-ending. In any society in which classes exist class struggle will never end. In classless society the struggle between the new and the old and between truth and falsehood will never end. In the fields of the struggle for production and scientific experiment, mankind makes constant progress and nature undergoes constant change; they never remain at the same level. Therefore, man has constantly to sum up experience and go on discovering, inventing, creating and advancing. Ideas of stagnation, pessimism, inertia and complacency are all wrong. They are wrong because they agree neither with the historical facts of social development over the past million years, nor with the historical facts of nature so far known to us (i.e. nature as revealed in the history of celestial bodies, the earth, life and other natural phenomena).

Quoted in "Premier Chou Enlai's Report on the Work of the Government to the First Session of the Third National Peoples' Congress of the People's republic of China" (December 21-22 1964). LRB 203.

Where do correct ideas come from? Do they drop from the skies? No. Are they innate of the mind? No. They come from social practice, and from it alone; they come from three kinds of social practice; the struggle for production, the class struggle and scientific experiments.

"Where Do Correct Ideas come from?" (May 1963),
1ˢᵗ pocket ed., p. 1. LRB 206.

> *Without preparedness superiority is not real superiority and there can be no initiative either. Having grasped this point, a force which is inferior but prepared can often defeat a superior enemy by surprise attack.*
>
> "On Protracted War" (May 1938), Selected Works,
> Vol II, pp. 165-66. LRB 98.
>
> *One-sidedness means thinking in terms of absolutes, that is, a metaphysical approach to problems. In the appraisal of our work, it is one-sided to regards everything either as all positive or as all negative . . . To regard everything as positive is to see only the good and not the bad, and to tolerate only praise and no criticism. To talk as though our work is good in every respect is at variance with the facts. It is not true that that everything is good; there are still shortcomings and mistakes. But neither is it true that everything is bad, and that, too is at variance with the facts. Here analysis is necessary. To negate everything is to think, without having made any analysis, that nothing has been done well and that the great work of socialist construction, the great struggle in which hundreds of millions of people are participating, is a complete mess with nothing in it worth commending. Although there is a difference between the many people who hold such views and those who are hostile to the socialist system, these views are very mistaken and harmful and can only dishearten people. It is wrong to appraise work either from the viewpoint that everything is positive, or from the viewpoint that everything is negative.*
>
> Speech at the Chinese Communist Party's National Conference
> on Propaganda Work (March 12, 1957) 1ˢᵗ pocket ed., pp. 16-17. LRB
> 219.

On the preceding pages I hope that I have been able to demonstrate that it is useful to apply Chairman Mao's wisdom to run a modern company. Let me just remind you about a few excerpts like: *"have a head for figures"*, *"grasp firmly"*, *"this is to take good care of cadres"*, *"learn to play the piano"*, *"Take the ideas of the masses and concentrate them"*, *"guard against arrogance"*, *"Exchange information"*, *"Ask your subordinates on matters that you do not understand"*, . . . *learn to look at problems allsidedly seeing the reverse as well as the obverse side"*, *"Fewer and better troops and simpler administration"*, *"The masses have boundless creative power"*, *". . . the most important question is the selection of a director and . . . . ", " . . . . but you must always remember not to be conceited . . . . "* just to mention a few of his many quotations. If you put them in the context of your own responsibility and adapt them to your own situation, you stand a solid chance to be a successful executive or to manage your company to great victories and a lot of success.

I am extremely satisfied with the fact that these old quotations combine wisdom and knowledge that may be applied today in a totally different setting. As I said in the introduction, just change words that were important during the Cultural Revolution with words that are important during the commercial revolution (like soldiers with employees, armies with companies, generals with general managers, etc.). To run a company is not very different from running a country as a political leader or to command an army during war, or being the coach of a soccer team or the conductor of a symphony orchestra. In all situations leadership has to be shown, and in all cases one has to command many different disciplines and skills. I hope that you agree with me that applying the philosophy of Chairman Mao to win a war or win the support of the population to a large extent is what is required to run a company where you fight your competitors, need loyal employees, analyze your financial figures, make and execute plans, etc.

Good luck with conquering the customers in the markets that you approach and with running a well-controlled company.

Reference and Literature

Title	Author	Date	Publisher
Quotations from Chairman Mao Tse Tung	Mao Tse Tung	1966	Foreign Language Press
Focus—Corporate Governance	Several	Fall 1997	Egon Zehnder International
Focus—Mastering Change	Several	Volume V/1 2001	Egon Zehnder International
Focus—Managing Integration	Several	Volume III, No 1	Egon Zehnder International
Focus—Managing Change in Global Enterprises	Several	Fall '98	Egon Zehnder International
Focus—Start-ups	Several	01/2000	Egon Zehnder International
Focus—Building Client Relationships	Several	Special Issue 2000	Egon Zehnder International
Forging Reform in China—The Fate of State-Owned Industry	Edward S. Steinfeld	First published 1998	Cambridge University Press

Time Trap—How to get more Done in Less Time	R. Alec Mackensie	1972	AMACOM
Opportunities—A Handbook of Business Opportunity Search	Edward de Bono	1980	Pelican Books
Business Conduct Guidelines			International Business Machines
Introduction to Business Dynamics			International Business Machines
How to Read a Financial Report			Merill Lynch Pierce Fenner & Smith Inc.
Amgen 2003 Annual Report			
Use your Head	Tony Buzan	1974	BBC Publications
Code of Conduct and Ethical Policies			Citicorp
Managing People at Work	John Hunt	1979	McGraw-Hill Book Company (UK) Ltd.
Reinventing the Factory II	Roy L. Harmon	1992	The Free Press—New York

In search of Excellence	Thomas J. Peters and Robert H. Waterman, jr.	1982	Harper & Row, Publishers, Inc.—New York
"Seeing the Future First"	by Gary Hamel and C. K. Prahaladad	Sept. 5,1994	Fortune magazine
Partnering for Value	The Performance Group		The Performance Group Meltzers gt. 4, N-0257 Oslo, Norway
Get Your Mission Statement Working	David L. Calfee	January 1993	Management Review
The seven habits of spectacularly unsuccessful executives.	Sydney Finkelstein	January/ February 2004	Article in Ivey Business Journal
Lincoln on Leadership	Donald T. Phillips II	1992	Warner Books Inc., 1271 Avenue of Americas, New York, NY 10020
Performance Drivers—A practical guide to using the balanced scorecard	Nils-Gøran Olve, Jan Roy and Magnus Wetter	2000	JohnWiley and Sons, Ltd

The Keys to Break Through Performance	Compiled by The Performance Group		The Performance Group Meltzers gt. 4, N-0257 Oslo, Norway
Corporate Director's Guidebook—2nd edit.		1994	American Bar Associations, 750 North Lakeshore Drive, Chicago, Illinois 60611
Review of The Northbound Train: Finding the Purpose, Setting the Direction, Shaping the Destiny of Your Organization—by Karl Albrecht	Ronald E. Yates wrote the review		
Magazines— Numerous ideas have come out of reading magazines and newspapers—notably Newsweek, USA Today, Dagens Næringsliv (Major Norwegian Business Daily) and Ukeavisen Ledelse (Norwegian weekly business newpaper and its daily website)—during the period that this book was written			

Internet—the websites
of many companies
and publications have
also been sources for
inspiration during the
period this book came to
fruition